THE HIDDEN TRIANGLE
A French Odyssey

GW00536537

THE HIDDEN TRIANGLE

A French Odyssey

VALERIE THOMPSON

ISBN
1 901253 32 5
First published June 2003

© Valerie Thompson

The moral right of Valerie Thompson to be identified as the author
of this work has been asserted by her in accordance with the
Copyright, Designs and Patents Act 1988.

All rights reserved. No part of this publication may be reproduced,
stored in a retrieval system, or transmitted in any form or by any
means, electronic, mechanical, photocopying, recording or
otherwise, without the prior permission of the publisher
and copyright owner.

Published by:
Léonie Press
an imprint of
Anne Loader Publications
13 Vale Road, Hartford,
Northwich, Cheshire CW8 1PL
Gt Britain
Tel: 01606 75660   Fax: 01606 77609
e-mail: anne@aloaderpubs.u-net.com
Website: www.anneloaderpublications.co.uk
www.leoniepress.com

Printed by:
Anne Loader Publications

Contents

List of illustrations

About the Author

Valerie Thompson trained as a teacher of Art and Music at Homerton College, Cambridge, too long ago to want to remember. After a brief but successful career in a Secondary Modern School, she worked for a short time on the Committee for Drug Addiction at the Department of Health.

A family followed and all but her singing was put to one side for a while. Later she took on the job of accompanying a local choir. Returning to paint at the Field Study Centre at Flatford Mill was a welcome relief from domestic duties. For a few years Valerie taught painting to adults on holiday courses there and elsewhere.

Creatively she has never let up, in spite of managing a large house and garden in England and taking on the French property as well. In her spare time Valerie has studied silversmithing, written numerous poems, composed many songs, a mass and a requiem, and travelled widely, as well as having fun hunting for bargains at antique fairs.

Aged 40 something, she returned to College to study Interior

Design and came away with an award and a distinction and started advertising her skills. However, this business has been very low-key, hence the time to write a book.

This, her first published book is not just about buying and restoring an old stone house in the Correze, but also about daily life there, memoirs, observations, nature, history, legends, cookery, the arts – a veritable *pot-pourri* of many of the things which fascinate her.

Dedication

To my husband Tony, who indulges my fanciful
francophile follies, and my girls and friends,
whose practical and emotional support has
ensured the success of my ventures.
V.T.

La Folie Verte – our house in the 'Hidden Triangle'

Chapter 1

THOSE WERE THE DAYS

It all began in Wales. Organised painting courses around England were all very well, but I came to the conclusion that I needed a different kind of break from routine family life. I wanted to be independent and to find somewhere more secluded for my painting week away. The first cottage I rented in Wales was simple, basic; actually a pre-fabricated bungalow, with a dramatic view towards Chirk Castle – wonderful for painting and I did manage to get two oils finished – but it rained (nearly all week!). The second, a former gatehouse to a big estate on the Lleyn peninsula, was charming, isolated and cosy. It needed to be cosy. I lit a log fire every evening I was there – in July! And it rained! The rain it raineth every day! One and a half pictures later and I'd had enough of Wales.

For some time I had been muttering about going abroad, on

1

my own, to paint. Finally, in 1986 I made up my mind to do it. France seemed the most practical option, as it was not too far for an inexperienced solo traveller to venture abroad for the first time. I spoke adequate French; I could get by with my rather rusty school-acquired language, last learnt in anger in 1960. My accent was, and remains, somewhat better than my knowledge of vocabulary, which leads to the occasional problem when I am understood rather better than I can comprehend the reply. My distinctly shaky grammar always gives the game away in the end. But I rattle on regardless, and as long as I get my message over, that's all that really matters, even if I have to stop sometimes in the middle of what I am saying and start again a different way because there is a crucial word that I don't know. The French claim that our attempts to speak their tongue with a slightly 'off' accent are as charming as we find a French person struggling with English. I find that hard to believe.

My father, who had taken holidays with my mother before the war to Belgium, the South of France and the Italian Riviera, driving a splendid SS car (the precursor to the Jaguar), used to appear confident about driving on the right on unfamiliar roads. I thought he was a fantastic role model, though I became rather more critical of his competence when I began driving myself. I have never forgotten the time he drove out of a T-junction into the path of another car, which screeched to a halt inches from us. I had been married just a few hours! I nearly didn't have a honeymoon, or a life, come to that.

We used to travel *en-famille* when I was a teenager, crushed together in a small Ford. Our first trip, to Paris in 1955, began after a long, winding, sick-making drive to Dover from Surrey (no M25 then) and onto a ferry where cars and lorries were loaded and offloaded in a net. We waited, desperately bored, for seemingly interminable hours, miserably hunched on bollards on the harbour-side as ours was almost the last car to be lifted out. After another few hours we arrived at our rented flat in the dark. Paris made a deep impression on me, forming my abiding love affair with France. It was my daily duty to buy the morning *baguettes*, whose hot ends were well chewed by the time I returned to the apartment. I nervously tried out my faltering fragments of French with local youngsters in the nearby park and seemed able to communicate well enough. During our three-week stay I absorbed so much of the city's geography that, when I went back for a holiday with a college friend seven years later, I remembered much of the Metro system and was able to take us effortlessly to many of the principal sights. Then, Hilary and I stayed in a small back-street hotel in the student quarter, near the Boulevard St Michel, and ate substantial subsidised meals at one of their college restaurants. To today's adventurous youth this would all seem very tame, but for us it was a revolution – to be abroad, anywhere, without the constant domination of post-war parents.

After the awful experience of our first ferry trip, the next year we grandly crossed the Channel in one of the wonderful small planes that used to fly out of Lydd, a tiny airfield in Kent. The planes took just three or four cars in their bellies. It was such a quick and convenient way to get to France, though not very economical, I imagine. Subsequently, the ferries were modernised and with the advent of the 'ro-ro' ships, crossing the Channel became faster and easier. However, the roads weren't up to much. In the mid 1950s, not so long after the war, some of the tank and bomb damage in Northern France had not been repaired and the main roads were unmodernised. Uneven, bumpy, cobbled roads, lethally slippery when wet with rain, bisected many villages. There were no motorways, of course, and our prized eau-de-nil 1948 Ford Prefect was very slow and stately. Journeys were not comfortable. My older brother was about six feet tall by the age of fourteen and took up most of the back-seat space with his unwieldy legs. On top of this discomfort both parents smoked continuously and kept the car windows tightly closed. My father hated the cold and always drove, winter and summer, wearing his favourite trilby. He even wore it on the beach. With his little moustache, hooded eyes, distinctly hooked nose and the habit of holding a cigarette between his thumb and middle finger, hot end towards his palm so he had to rotate his hand to take a puff, he closely resembled a Chicago Mafia boss. At the Approved School where he taught delinquent teenage boys, this characteristic gesture earned him the nickname 'The Gangster'.

However uncomfortable the journeys were, however hot, tired, itchy from sitting on scratchy fabric seats and half-choked with the smoke, we tried not to complain. We knew that few people travelled abroad at that time (inexpensive package holidays hadn't yet been invented). Not many people even owned a car, so we were grateful for the chance to see beyond England's shores. Each year we went to Antibes on the Côte d'Azur, Ventimiglia on the Italian Riviera or Cesenatico on the Adriatic coast. I map-read and had responsibility for packing the car – good practice for my later trips. And it was packed – stuffed, in fact – as the four of us were usually away for three weeks. So much junk.

After the Ford, my father bought an old A70 estate-car conversion, nicknamed 'The Tank' because of the massive iron girder which had been used to make the back bumper. Its greatest luxury was the shiny leatherette bench seats, front and back, which could accommodate three at a pinch. And we could get in more junk. Some of it was tucked under a web of tapes we nailed to the wooden struts of the roof, or beneath the seats. All this preparation was necessary because at that time the journey to the South of France or Italy took two and a half days, with two overnight stops, and the family might require any of their belongings at any time. I was expected to know where everything was stowed.

Apart from our clothes, towels, linen and the usual holiday paraphernalia, there were other more unusual things we took to keep us occupied. My brother was a keen model aeroplane maker, designing and constructing planes from balsa wood and dope-painted tissue paper. I can never forget the pungent smell of dope, like a stronger version of clear nail varnish, as he painted it on to make the paper more taut and strong. Neither would my mother forget the way he ruined her built-in wooden ironing table in the scullery of our home in Surrey, with his pins, scalpel blades and balsa glue. Each summer he ended up making a boat with a tiny engine, instead of a plane. He also took a small can of fuel, which needed to be boosted with extra ether. I was more interested in using his ether to asphyxiate locusts, which I caught in a large handkerchief, pinning them out on some of his spare balsa wood to show their bright turquoise blue or luminous pink underwings. Another obscure space-filler was a huge black inner tube from a lorry, which my father inflated with the hand pump from the car. Everyone took turns to sit in it, floating luxuriantly on the sea, paddling around with our hands. It was fine as long as you kept your sunburnt thighs away from the sharp protruding valve.

We literally took everything but the kitchen sink. My mother even used to pack tins of stew for our suppers, which she heated up on the primitive two-ring camping-gaz burners provided at the camp sites where we stayed in wooden cabins no bigger than a garden shed. I can only remember peeling spuds, but we must have eaten other vegetables, and surely we bought the deliciously succulent local peaches for pudding. What is clear in my mind is the terrible rough red wine we all drank, mine mixed half-and-half with water and often 'improved' with a spoonful of sugar. My mother claimed that the wine acted as a disinfectant for the water, which was why I was allowed it aged only 12 or so. It never rained, at least not in my memory, so our meals were eaten outside at a table no bigger than one used for cards, with rocky folding chairs perched on the tiny gritty terrace. Inside the sheds there were four basic bunks and a line to hang up our clothes, not a lot else. My mother loved to dress up in the evenings with her little gold sandals and belt to match and join the parade of the rich and fashionable along the promenade at Juan les Pins or among the crowds in Antibes. I feel sure she wished that we children were not in tow: me always untidy and overweight, and my brother frequently scowling with boredom.

My father appeared to deal confidently, if irritably, with all the other small or large difficulties we encountered en route. There were usually some problems, but they never seemed insoluble – we always got there and back, eventually. The Austin was never the most reliable of cars. One year the radiator seized up due to rust falling into the pipes. Every 100 miles or so it would reach boiling point. The car steamily crawled through virtually deserted villages. There was never anyone to ask for help, so we'd search avidly for hand-cranked water pumps that actually worked, to fill the radiator yet again. Another year my father cautiously descended from the crest of the Simplon Pass into Italy with perilously defective brakes. Something vital had fallen off near the top, so we glided into a little rural garage at the bottom where a cheerful mechanic efficiently made and fitted a new part. Another time it was the big-end bearings (whatever they are) which failed. All I recall about this episode was the persistent knocking noise the car made, over many hundreds of miles. I was blissfully unaware of the dangers this old banger posed for us, and was just frustrated by losing some of our valuable holiday time. Typical teenage reaction.

A few years before my potentially momentous decision to take my first foreign holiday alone, I drove briefly in the South of France. Tony, my husband, and I were visiting one of his clients. She wanted to talk business with Tony and I wanted to go to Nice, so I was offered the client's left-hand drive car to take myself off for a few hours. Negotiating the sharp bends of the narrow coast road and the even narrower back alleys of Nice in an unfamiliar car, on the wrong side of both the car and the road, was a daunting prospect. However, my success in returning myself and the car in one piece gave me the confidence to believe that I could drive myself to France in my own familiar car.

Cinois windmill
Vr 2002

Chapter 2

SEEDS

I tried not to recall the motoring misadventures of my youth when I set out for France that summer. Friends and relatives were more anxious than my immediate family (who must have had faith in my ability to extricate myself from awkward scrapes).

"What if you get lost?" they asked, "or break down?"

But I had no real qualms. There were no mobile phones yet for emergencies, but I had maps and I was feeling intrepid, however tame it may now seem to young backpackers who casually fly off to all parts of the world with no idea of where they'll be staying. For me, this *was* an adventure.

Boarding the ferry at Dover caused me no difficulty, neither did the sea-crossing. After an easy run of about 200 miles I stopped at a family-run hotel in Les Andeleys, a small pretty town west of Paris. Showered and changed, I went down for dinner. I treated myself to an *apéritif*, a good meal, coffee and brandy, and the whole bill – meal, room and breakfast – came to under £20! Those were the days. After dinner I drove a few miles (over the limit, I guess), to the dramatic ruins of Chateau Gaillard, high on a cliff overlooking a sweeping bend in the Seine. I sat on a fallen stone, among a myriad of wild flowers and watched the sun setting, deep red and gold reflected in the river. My whole being felt a great contentment and peace, as if I had come home. I vividly remember thinking, "Yes, this is where I want to be, right now." I felt very self-satisfied with my decision to take this trip. Everything was going so well.

Reading afterwards about ancient Chateau Gaillard, (Gaillard meaning 'brave', 'saucy' or 'petulant' according to various interpretations), I came across several stories of violence and cruelty perpetrated there. Richard I of England, also called Richard the Lionheart, or Coeur de Lion in France (where he was equally well known), had taken part in the bloody Third Crusade to Jerusalem to fight against the powerful leader, Saladin, whom he defeated in two battles. Although Richard did not capture Jerusalem he made a deal with Saladin to allow Christians to visit the city. Legend has it that he was travelling home in disguise but this pretence was not clever enough to prevent him from being captured by Duke Leopold of Austria. Blondel, the famous troubadour, on hearing Richard singing within his prison, responded with a familiar tune. He then reported back Richard's whereabouts to England. His mother dispatched two Abbots to scour Europe in search of him. It's a good story but the facts of his return were sadly quite prosaic. Leopold passed Richard over to The Holy Roman Emperor, Henry VI, who returned him to England once an enormous ransom, collected by his English subjects, had been paid.

Shortly after his return to England, Richard set off again to defend the English-owned northern part of France. He was responsible for constructing Chateau Gaillard in 1197 at a cost of £8,000, a considerable sum at that time. As the castle is in an extremely good defensive position, dominating the river Seine and its traffic, it was a vital strategic link in the control of Normandy. Everyone wanted it and many were prepared to fight and die for it. However Richard didn't own it for long. Hearing that a peasant had found some gold statues and coins in a field, the greedy and poverty-stricken Richard disputed their ownership with the local Feudal Lord of the Manor. Besieging the village near Châlus he was shot in the shoulder by an arrow from a new type of crossbow. It is said that he even acknowledged the marksman with a wave, for his accurate bowmanship. The wound, left untreated at Richard's insistence, went septic and he died shortly afterwards. Richard's henchmen, when they captured the castle, hanged all the defenders except the talented archer, who was flayed alive. Although Chateau Gaillard was almost impregnable, King Philip Augustus of France finally overcame the resident English opposition on March 6th 1204, it is said, by sending in troops through the latrine shafts.

Some years ago I discovered another story – this one rather more gruesome – about Chateau Gaillard. The tale belies the present-day sense of idyllic calm at the placid empty site. Louis X, King of France, also known as Louis le Hutin (the Quarrelsome or the Headstrong), was married to the beautiful young aristocrat, Marguerite de Bourgogne. In 1314 he accused her of infidelity with two of his Knights and at the trial they were all found guilty. Almost certainly it was a trumped-up charge. Louis had previously failed in his attempt to annul their marriage in order to take another wife. Marguerite was imprisoned in Chateau Gaillard and was strangled, probably on Louis's orders, the following year at the tender age of only 25. The Knights were also executed.

Louis remarried in August 1315, only months after Marguerite's death. His new wife was Clemence of Hungary, but Louis didn't live to see their child, a son and his successor, as he died in 1316. Serves him right! More poignant is that his

9

son only lived a few months and was succeeded by Louis X's brother. For the next few hundred years the castle passed from France to England and back again until the 16th century, when it came under prolonged and intense attack during the Wars of Religion. King Henry IV of France eventually succeeded in ousting the English defenders and then decided to demolish most of the fortifications. After the efficient efforts of his troops, little remains apart from one complete tower and some other broken remnants of the walls and the keep. The abandoned ruins on their high cliff now seem romantic, their turbulent past long forgotten.

Early the next morning I visited Monet's magical garden at Giverny, which he planned and developed for over 40 years. Its tunnels of scented roses and vibrant herbaceous beds, with their riotously clashing colours and brilliant hues, have been kept just as he painted them. Sadly, neither the wisteria on the Japanese bridge, nor the famous pale waterlilies he painted so obsessively, were in bloom as it was too early in the year. The hazy early morning light created an atmosphere of mystery around the house and floral alleys, where one could almost sense the ghosts of the ponderous rotund painter and his lively family. Imagination filled in the colours we think we know so well. Except, of course, one can never truly know and certainly not begin to imitate the colours Monet used. Close examination of any of his pictures shows layers of the most unexpected shades and tints as well as pure colours, applied unmixed.

All of the loosely associated group of artists, known later as the Impressionists, tried to depict fleeting effects of light, working on the spot, mainly out of doors, though their still-life paintings tended to be done in the studio. Earlier painters had not worked this way. Previously, most artists had taken notes and done quick colour sketches, then brought these into the studio to work on, producing highly finished paintings using very formal techniques of design and structure. The Impressionists' spontaneous approach to their work gives a looser and freer effect. However, Monet was a slow worker and often took the unfinished paintings back to his studio where he continued, sometimes for months, superimposing layer upon layer of paint on his canvases. They still give us the sense of impromptu inspiration, quickly executed. Monet kept several canvases primed and moved from one to another as the light changed. He chose several local views to paint over and over again at different times of the day. Most memorable of the series of paintings he did in France are the poplars by the river, the haystacks and Rouen Cathedral, of which he did at least thirty in the space of only two years, between 1892 and 1894. Monet also stayed for a while at the Savoy in London, painting the Thames and the Houses of Parliament. Sometimes he was rowed in a little boat to the middle of the river in order to get just the right angle for a picture. Failing eyesight in his later years probably accounts for the increasingly abstract nature of his work, the waterlilies becoming mere streaks of paint without much underlying form. Most popular, since his death, proved to be those charming fields of corn and poppies, with bonnet and bustle-clad ladies out for a summer walk with their scampering children, that are now immortalised in popular culture as posters and greetings cards. I wandered up and down the pathways lined with exuberant planting, thinking about the paintings I knew Monet had done at Giverny and the joy he had had in making his spectacular and tranquil garden, now open for the pleasure of all and sundry.

After all the visual stimulation of the garden, I was surprised to find much of his house dark, almost gloomy, furnished as he had left it with some of the walls almost completely obscured by the Japanese prints he loved. The startling exception was the kitchen, boldly decorated in strong yellow and blue, a colour combination which has influenced many interior designers in the late twentieth century. His china, with its bright concentric bands, has been copied over and over again. Outside, the house is painted in candy pink, the shutters a soft mid-green, possibly to complement some of the more subtle coloured flowers. There are several paintings where Monet used his house as a background. In the Musée d'Orsay in Paris is a lovely picture called 'Luncheon'; a table covered with a white cloth has been left uncleared after the family have finished their alfresco lunch; children, probably his own, with their mother, can be seen playing in the garden near the house. Nothing seems to have changed from the time the picture was done to the present. I had this stunning garden almost to myself, having arrived even before the ticket office was open, and with a certain smugness, I left, passing coach-loads of tourists, soon to fill that still place of memories and ghosts with brash chatter and movement.

Cinais, a little farming village near Chinon, was my destination for my week away. The house was not very easy to find as the brochure had described the cottage as being opposite white farm gates. All the farms had white gates and the photo of the property had been taken from the back, just to confuse! However, once found, I settled into a delightful, if very simple, one-up, one-down house, almost trogloditic, as the ground floor was built right against a low vertical hillside, though it wasn't excavated from the rock. French doors opened from the upper landing onto some grass at first floor level. At the front was a small stony but flower-filled garden and views to a neglected windmill exactly on the skyline. Heaven! Painting went well. I did a few small oils, several pen and ink drawings around the house and village, and a watercolour or two.

On dull-weather days I visited some of the nearby historic sites. Not far away was the ruined mediæval chateau of Chinon, high on a bluff, commanding the town and river far below. There, I asked another visitor to take my photo in the bare round tower room, notable as the site of the fateful first meeting between Joan of Arc and the Dauphin. I discovered another royal connection with Chinon, for it was here that Henry II died in 1170, having been defeated in a battle against his own son and heir, Richard Lionheart – the same Richard of Chateau Gaillard fame, or infamy (more of him later). The jettied timber-framed house, much restored, in which Henry died, still stands on one of the main streets of the town. Below the chateau are caves, really *caves* (as in the French for 'wine-store') as they are full of the wines locally produced by Plouzeau et Fils. I thoroughly enjoyed a *dégustation* and came back another year, having failed to find their wine distributed in France, let alone England, to buy my favourite, BelleAmour, which I discovered on this first trip. On the second occasion I had forgotten my preferred vintage and asked for a tasting. The first I set to one side. The second was the right one. I have rarely seen such a look of amazement, as French viticulturists do not expect the English – and especially English women – to know much about wine!

Another day I went to the romantic Renaissance Chateau of Ussé, which probably influenced the author Perrault for his story of The Sleeping Beauty. Pretty tableaux depict the story in several of Ussé's magical conical fairy-tale towers, where life-sized wax figures, in decorative silks and lace-trimmed period costume, delight visitors of all ages. One peers in through the open windows around the towers, while carefully negotiating a narrow machiolated walkway high above the ground. It's not as dangerous as it sounds – there are no gaps in the floor for the pouring of boiling oil on unwelcome visitors, as might have been found in earlier castles. Ussé was not built for defence, only for enjoyment.

For a mixture of the solemn and fanciful I also visited the 11th and 12th century Abbey of Fontevraud, burial place of King Henry II and his wife Eleanor of Aquitaine, also of the ubiquitous Richard the Lionheart, and Isabelle, widow of King John. Their sculpted and painted tombs, probably empty since being desecrated in the Revolution, are remarkably well preserved, with much original paint still surviving. My abiding memory of this wonderful range of monastic buildings is the huge eight-sided kitchen, much restored and elaborated during the 19th century. It sports twenty chimneys and twenty fireplaces and an enormous spire, the whole looking like some misshapen pineapple with its stone roof and chimneys carved into small pyramids.

Another afternoon I visited the mediæval home of Rabelais, rustically reconstructed as it might have been in his lifetime. Here he is thought to have written *Gargantua* and *Pantagruel*. How appropriate his flamboyant writing about food and the wilder excesses of life seemed, even after five centuries, in that area of lush farmland and abundance. And how appropriate that BelleAmour wine, which I had so enjoyed one evening. I was in love.

On one fine evening I attended a *son et lumière* at the chateau of Azay le Rideau, another Renaissance treasure house, where local people acted out scenes from its history. Much of the French commentary was inaudible or incomprehensible, but the magical atmosphere in the crisp evening light, together with the music and graceful dancing, carried me along. One did not need to understand in order to be entertained. The performance began at dusk and finished in the dark, when the gentlemen of the troupe slowly rowed the elegant ladies, in their flowing mediæval-style dresses of silks and velvets, across the torch-lit moat to the sound of ethereal music. This was more than love. I was enchanted, overwhelmed, captivated.

One day I phoned home, excited about a good oil painting I had just finished. It depicted the sweeping curve of the river, the lower town, and the Chateau of Chinon dominating the crest of the hill, with an impressionist's sky; white, fluffy clouds slowly drifting across a strong blue.

"What, you've been out painting today?" said Tony, astonished. "It's been pouring all the time here."

Even the weather had conspired to charm me, and the painting I did that day hangs permanently on our living room wall. It is one I have consistently refused to sell, as it brings back such happy memories of a most important and meaningful time of my life.

Chinon supported several estate agents, and, while browsing around the attractive shops one day, I couldn't help but see how amazingly cheap the properties were, compared with English prices. They ranged from £10,000 for something needing total repair and restoration to about £30,000 for a three-bedroom house already restored. My tiny rented cottage was fine for a brief holiday, but it lacked home comforts. There was no armchair or sofa (a typical feature of French-owned *gîtes*, I later discovered). There was no proper cooker, only a microwave and, bleakly, no lampshade on the bedroom's central light-bulb. I made a shade from some of my drawing paper, pleating it into a double fan, taped together, and suspended it from some string. But the other things the cottage lacked were less easy to remedy! I started to think how nice it would be to have a real home-from-home with comfortable furniture, the walls decorated attractively in clear bright colours instead of the typically French brown and orange, nice china, lampshades – a home made truly homely with inexpensive and amusing *bric-à-brac*. The only way I could have all that was to buy my own holiday home.

All autumn and winter I chuntered on about France, French property, French food and even French weather. I was becoming quite a bore on the subject. Friends even started asking Tony when and where we were buying our French house. His firm reply was, "We're not." But I requested brochures from French property agencies in England who had representatives in France, at first looking at them secretly, then more brazenly as Tony became more accustomed to the idea. Eventually, though still somewhat reluctantly, he was won over.

"As long as I don't have to do any of the work," he said. "You get it organised and deal with the builders and I'll get a loan from the Bank."

The seeds had been successfully sown.

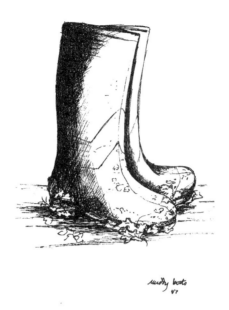

muddy boots
VT

Chapter 3

HUNTING

My next decision was, where in France did I want my house? It is an enormous country, and I had at that time only seen small parts of the north and northwest, the south, the Loire region and Paris. Although I had enjoyed my short stay at Cinais, I didn't find the countryside particularly stimulating for painting. It was too flat. The chateaux were fabulous, but as I mainly paint domestic buildings in the landscape, rocks and flowers, the area did not seem to have long-term appeal. I started reading any books, articles or brochures I could find about France, its diverse departments, its landscape, climate, over-run tourist areas and places to avoid. I discovered that the weather was usually warmer south of the Loire. It seemed a good idea to find something just one day's travel from the coast to avoid an overnight stop. Many areas were too flat, too isolated, too industrial… but something, I knew, would suddenly 'speak' to me. It did. When I read Freda White's excellent book "Three Rivers of France" (now in an attractive illustrated reprint), I had found my destination. She described an area of great beauty, tranquillity, history and, as yet, not discovered by mass tourism or too many English holiday-home owners. 'The Hidden Triangle' she called it. By an extraordinary quirk of luck, during our previous summer holiday in Corsica, I had made friends with one of the staff whose parents, I discovered by chance, owned a house in France. I had taken their name and address, "Just in case," I had said, and now found that their place was exactly in the middle of the area I wanted to explore. We made contact and I arranged to rent their property for ten days over the Easter holidays. Now I was ready to make appointments to meet agents in France. I booked the ferry for my elder daughter, Pippa, her best friend Louise ('Lulu') and myself, and declared my intention to go house-hunting.

We nearly didn't make it, as there was a strike at several French ports that Easter. With only a week to go and with the strikers obviously digging their heels in about whatever it was that they wanted, I began to think we would never get away. We were extraordinarily lucky to obtain the last slot on the 9am hovercraft on Easter Saturday! I had invited both of my girls, but Vicky decided not to join us, so we were just three intrepid women setting off into the unknown. Blois, in the Loire district, was our overnight stopping place as we had chosen a short sea route and a long drive, rather than the other way round. Tony pessimistically predicted that on Easter Saturday we'd struggle to find a hotel and we'd all have to sleep in the car. But the second hotel we tried offered us a three-bedded room with bath for £21, and from the balcony we had a view of the magnificent chateau.

France takes great civic pride in its town centres, filling them with flowers, sculpture and fountains, and Blois was no exception. After dinner we walked along the riverside, admiring the beautifully floodlit old buildings. Ice creams were an indulgence at a lively popular café, frequented by the young, old and all in-between. Now the girls were hooked too. Envious of the easy relaxed way everyone sat around, chatting and drinking coffee, beer, or soft drinks, they wanted to be a part of this way of life. They wanted to belong.

Travelling with Louise was not always easy. She had a strong aversion to the 'stand and deliver' loos still prevalent in many bars and restaurants around France. Many a day she had to keep her legs crossed for quite a time while we searched for suitable conveniences. She was not comfortable with the idea of squatting behind a hedge either. Nowadays most loos have been modernised, even becoming so streamlined that some-times it is difficult to find the flush. There are so many varia-tions: a button on top, one on the floor, an automatic flow as you close the lid, paper seat covers at the touch of a switch, but all these wonders came too late for poor Lulu. She also had a noisy detestation of water towers, which she found unbearably ugly, and screamed out in horror every time she saw one. We got used to these outbursts. We had to.

I was eager to see the countryside and towns I had only known about from written descriptions. Deciding to take the Le Mans-Poitiers-Limoges route was rather a slow way to do a long journey, as the road had few sections of dual carriageway, let alone any motorway. Approaching Limoges, a tortuous town to negotiate, the scenery started to change, becoming more interesting, hilly and wooded. Superbly engineered bridges appeared to fly over deep valleys. One overlooks the romantically-sited village of Pierre-Buffière, with its higgledy-piggledy development on top of a steep hill. It's lovely to look at from the road, but the inhabitants' idyllic view has been ruined by the enormous bridge.

The road plunges down an immensely long hill to the valley of the Vezère, and up the other side through pretty, historic Uzerche. The pounding lorries must cause awful pollution as they ponderously, painfully grind up the steep hill. We too, had to patiently crawl through Uzerche before taking the road to Tulle, a straggly charmless town in a dark sombre valley. Tulle is most often remembered locally for a dreadful wartime atrocity. On 8th June 1944 the *maquis* overcame the occupying Germans, but the very next day the town was retaken by the German soldiers. In retribution 99 local Resistance members were hanged from lamp-posts and many people were deported, 101 of them never to return. A memorial to the victims was erected beside the road to the south. Tulle's church and fine cloisters, and a small area of old alleys and houses in the *Englos* or enclosure, are the only attractive features to relieve its oppressive gloom. The winding road crosses and re-crosses the river. Signposts are few and far between, but with Pippa's map-reading skills stretched to their limits, we emerged eventually from its seemingly endless streets to climb a long hill towards our chosen territory.

The landscape just got better and better. Stone houses and farms are of subdued colour, roofed with handmade tiles or slate, sometimes cut conventionally into oblongs, but often prettily trimmed into shell shapes. Stones, locally known as *lauze*, are also chiselled into shell-like curves to cover the more traditional buildings. *Lauze* is immensely heavy, as much as one ton per square metre if used in the ancient way – overlapping deeply and built into the very walls of the house. Think of the substantial timber rafters that must support this enormous weight. Red handmade clay tiles are sometimes flat, or curved, as in the Roman-style pantiles. A few houses have been re-roofed with modern materials, with concrete slabs or factory-produced clay tiles, too regular for our desire for the picturesque. Farm and village houses look as if they have grown from the very ground itself, as they are mostly of local stone of various colours, some golden, others grey and some truly red. Those which have decayed badly, or are more recent and cheaply built of breeze blocks or curious pierced building blocks made of hard-baked tile clay, are often covered with *crêpi*, a long-lasting tinted cement rendering. Sometimes this rendering makes it quite difficult to distinguish the old from the new, so the little hamlets have a greater sense of unity than our patchily developed villages. Most houses have good-sized shuttered windows and the older ones often have solid stone steps leading up to a covered porch or balcony on first floor level, which would have been the main access to the living quarters when animals were still housed on the ground floor. This smelly idea of animal husbandry had the advantage of providing some underfloor heating in the winter.

The trees were dressed in spring green and irises flourished at the roadside, presaging our arrival in the hidden triangle. Some late fruit trees were still in blossom and the sunshine added a generally festive air to the little towns and villages we passed. From one point, about ten miles from our destination, we had a long view eastwards to the mountains of the Auvergne, still tipped with snow. It was a quite unexpected and breathtaking sight. So far, I was not disappointed by my choice of region.

Some more tricky map-reading and inspired guesswork led us to the tiny hamlet where we had rented a house. Oh dear! The track from the lane ran with water from an uncontrolled spring. Wellie boots were a necessity. Thank goodness we had brought them. The entrance, a right-angled bend between the house and a barn, was too narrow for the car. Backing cautiously out into the lane again, I parked mid-stream then squelched up and down the track, across a quagmire of spongy moss where the stream sank into the earth, with bags and boxes, which we deposited on the dry side of the house. Keys were collected from the neighbouring farm, where, we were told – after all this effort – we could have parked in a dry yard and used their dry path to approach the house. We could have done with that information a little earlier!

Eventually, after trying each of the four doors with all of the keys, one was made to fit. A good shove, and then… flies, millions of flies, mostly dead, but some still buzzing or twitching or spinning in dizzy circles on the floor. As we were the first to use the house since the previous summer we had to deal with the horrible problem. The door was quickly slammed shut and after a further hour, having yet again tried all the keys with greater success, we managed to get into the kitchen to find some fly spray. A frenzied flurry of spraying, with scarves tightly tied around our mouths and noses, was followed by a mammoth clean-up operation. Every corner of the room which was to be the girls' bedroom had to be swept and dusted before bed-making and supper could be started.

Exploring further we found a modern newly fitted bathroom upstairs. However, the instructions for the water-heater were vague, and the water remained lukewarm for the whole of our stay. The local plumber never answered our calls, though he has become a firm friend since, doing extensive work for us over the years (and nearly always comes when we phone him... eventually). In the kitchen we found that waste water from the original stone sink poured directly through a hole pierced in the wall, with no apparent drain to take it away. Unmatching and cracked mugs and plates confirmed my determination to make my own home as appealing as possible, with matching china, a functioning bathroom and cheerful decorative schemes.

The roof space had wonderful potential for several bedrooms, but in the 10 years the owners had used the house the conversion had never been done. Old blankets had been roughly pinned up to divide the loft into tent-like sleeping spaces. The two bedrooms were downstairs, occupying the rooms which ought to have been a fine sitting room with lovely views from its generous windows, and a sizeable dining room. As it was, all living happened in the kitchen, which had an open fireplace. This was a true blessing. Three feet from the log fire was the only warm spot in the house. There was a portable gas heater by which we dressed and undressed, one at a time, standing right in front of it – but we felt uneasy about leaving it on all night, so we slept with tights under our pyjamas and a jumper over the top, and loaded the beds with as many blankets as we could find. In spite of the house's limitations we loved it, going out each day, house-hunting or sightseeing, then coming back for supper and comfortable chats, companionably poring over plans, maps and magazines.

I had asked the English agents to send me particulars of possible properties with a top price of £25,000 and had selected, from the often grey and indistinct photos, a few I thought worth seeing. The first agent I had arranged to meet was Anne, an English lady living about 15 miles from our base. From the start we were easy and compatible; she was great fun and sympathetic to my requirements. Her own house has the sort of character we were looking for – stone construction, on different levels, a modest garden and a view. Over coffee we discussed the houses in her portfolio that were within my price range. I had received a few photos and descriptions from her London agency and had picked out several which I thought we should look at. Anne agreed with my selection and offered a few more she now had on her books. She re-read my initial letter with gales of laughter, as she remembered that I was the lady who had requested a *boulangerie* within easy walking distance for my breakfast bread as one of my main priorities. Never mind the number of bedrooms, or whether it was on mains drainage, just a *boulangerie*. Pippa commented to Anne's son, a doctor, who was busy mending a pair of trousers, that she hoped he didn't sew up his patients so crudely. This was greeted with more hoots of laughter, and on that jolly note we sallied forth.

For two days we trekked around a wide area looking at some truly bizarre houses. Having asked to see one that needed everything doing to it, Anne showed us a wreck with walls and a roof but little else, costing £10,000. I really felt I couldn't cope with a total restoration project, not living 500 miles away, and anyway, it would probably have cost more to reconstruct to a reasonable standard than to buy one mostly done up already. Some of the houses had extraordinary features, like the one near Martel, last lived in by an old lady, who had had a loo installed in her bedroom. Good idea! But not right in the middle of the room! We rejected that one, not in fact because of the aberrant loo but because the house was dull and the locality boring. Another reject was 'The Railway House', so-named by us because it was right next to a railway line – admittedly little used. Its view across the valley was marred by an illegal rubbish tip spilling down the opposite slope. In fact, it was a handsome house, with a grand central staircase leading to a galleried landing and spacious bedrooms. If only we could have picked it up and moved it somewhere else.

The next was very isolated, with definitely no nearby *boulangerie*, its setting spoiled by a big concrete and asbestos barn immediately opposite. Another was sweet, pretty, but semi-detached, too small with not enough privacy. We were getting more choosy the more we saw. Then there was the partly-completed barn conversion, probably designed by an amateur (maybe the owner), as many of the ideas were out of keeping with the building itself and quite impractical. There were staircases cutting across doorways, and a small mezzanine floor with no obvious purpose, not big enough for a bedroom and too public for a quiet study or reading room. One little house had a lot of charm, but not much else as the kitchen could only accommodate one person – no use for the communal cooking I enjoyed with the girls. Enquiring as to the whereabouts of the advertised three bedrooms, we were shown two in the roof, accessed by a home-made ladder. They had no windows at all! We weren't doing very well, but at least it was confirming in our minds what we wanted and, more often, what we didn't.

This catalogue of unsuitable properties did not deter or depress us, because on the first day we had seen, in the late afternoon, the house that was eventually to become ours. It was the most conventional, sound and almost liveable, and it had great potential. Anything we saw after this one was compared to it, "This one doesn't have… the other one was…"

We knew we had found it. It had spoken to us, just like the description of the *département* in Freda White's book, and it was right in the middle of the area I had pinpointed from my research at home. However, I dutifully kept my appointments with other agents. One, who took us to see properties in the Lot, showed us nothing of great interest, though it is a beautiful *département* and there are many lovely houses. Maybe our budget wouldn't stretch to the nice ones and we didn't want to penetrate too far south into the Lot as it would have been too far for my stipulated 'one day's journey from the coast'. On the fourth day, after a very early start, I drove along the River Dordogne to meet an agent based to the west of Bergerac. What a wasted day that proved to be, apart from an excellent lunch, as the agent failed to turn up at the agreed time and we didn't like the area anyway. The further west we went the less it pleased us as the landscape near the river was too flat and the villages too tidy. All the gardens were manicured, the stonework of the houses too meticulously repointed, and the paintwork too immaculate – all too English! It was, as we learned later, popular English territory and there appeared to be a lot of 'keeping up with the Joneses'. We wanted something more rustic, more typically French.

The following day the three of us returned to our preferred house to have a more thorough look around, to assess what work was necessary and to take some measurements, mainly so that we could work out how to extend into the loft. On telling the curious old lady next door that I was considering buying the house, she declared, enthusiastically, "How charming! How pleased I will be to have you as neighbours." What a welcome! We were in love again.

Tony was informed of our choice and, still slightly reluctant, gave the go-ahead. He agreed to approach the bank, initially for £25,000, which was the un-negotiable price of the house. Then he would have to find more for legal fees, which are peculiarly devised in France, as they are calculated on a sliding scale. Strangely, a cheaper property costs more for the legal transactions than does a more expensive one. The purchaser also pays all the legal expenses, so the cost works out at nearly 10 per cent more than the advertised price. Anne was told of our decision, which she thought was brave as there seemed such a lot in the way of improvements to do, and she knew we were intending to do as much as we could ourselves. The lawyer, the *notaire*, was seen and papers drawn up to give Anne a Power of Attorney to sign documents in our absence. We had to produce marriage and birth certificates and made many other declarations as to our status and relations before things could go ahead. As the elderly French owner of the house, Monsieur Coruble, lived near the Pyrenees, several hours' drive away, with his daughter, who was negotiating on his behalf, we did not meet to sign the initial agreement, nor indeed to sign the final papers. Unusually a 10 per cent deposit was not demanded. Once the decision had been made I tried to move quickly. I didn't want Tony to change his mind. I was well on my way to joining the hordes of English property owners in France.

Chapter 4
LA FOLIE VERTE

La Folie Verte, as I subsequently named the solid stone house, was not perfect in every respect, although it had some pretty features, such as the shell-shaped slate roof tiles. The previous owner, a widower, had defiled its rustic simplicity with some horrendous 1950s 'improvements'. For a start, there was a hideous enclosed porch of glass and metal, like a tall greenhouse, right at the front. This would have to be the first thing to go. How planning permission had ever been given to put on this grotesque accretion I will never understand, as the whole village is a conservation area. Improvements and changes, as I subsequently discovered, are not always approved. But there definitely seemed to be one law for the locals and one for strangers. Some of the houses and barns have been repaired with exposed breeze blocks and

corrugated iron or plastic, without any thought for the aesthet-
ic effect of such materials. Then there was the oil store, with
one wall of bamboo, one of breeze blocks and the whole roofed
with corrugated plastic, firmly in the public eye. This, I
planned, would be the second improvement, though this was
not to be. Replacing this ugly, ramshackle lean-to became quite
a battle.

Inside, the narrow stairs, inserted between the main structural beams, had just a few banisters set at right angles to the
rail, which made one feel quite seasick to look at. An ancient
cracked sink, just to the left of the entrance, graced the large
kitchen/dining room, which was illuminated by a pair of double French doors at the front and one small barred window.
This window has a chain attached to the frame and a hook on
the wall, effectively allowing it to be left open for ventilation
(useful when the cooker was installed beneath it). I guess it
probably dates from the time when this room was used to
house animals. One wall supported the ugliest over-ornate
dresser ever seen. That would be the third thing to disappear,
and a window needed to be created on this long blank wall,
which would then have a lovely view over the cherry trees. A
self-contained boiler room would prove invaluable for drying
towels and clothes as its oil-fed boiler (once regulated, with
some tender loving care and lots of money) not only provided
constant hot water and heated several radiators, but also the
little boiler room itself.

Off the kitchen, a scruffy lobby with a few shelves led to an
adequately equipped bathroom, though improvements could
be made here too. The floor needed replacing as did the shower fittings. The window, which could not be opened, was made
of reeded glass cubes, a building material I have always dis-
liked intensely. I found out that the former owner had put it in,
very crudely, making a nasty mess of the mortar between the
exterior stones. The reason for a window that didn't open and
that was made of opaque glass was to become clearer when we
attempted to get permission to insert the window in the

kitchen. Monsieur Coruble had not owned the land on that side of the house and neither did we. The law states that in order to put in a window one has to own the land over which it opens, or obtain the owner's permission.

Upstairs, the living room struck us as the finest feature. It is a huge room, with three windows looking over the village, the valley and the hillside behind the house. The ceiling is very high, with great rough chestnut beams. There was an original stone sink set into the wall, with a working tap, just like at our rented house, except that there was a drainpipe outside this one. Bizarrely, here, the alcove was painted bright red inside! Fortunately the stonework, which formed shelves either side of the opening, was untouched. Repainting the walls inside this attractive feature was number five on the growing list of essential improvements. Then there was the enormous inglenook fireplace, which had been all but massacred by the old man. The flue from the boiler below had been brutally thrust through the floor of the hearth, straight up the existing chimney, thus ruining its use as an open fire. What is more, he had covered the boiler flue with hollow breeze blocks, rendered all the stonework of the rear and side walls and covered the supporting and lintel beams with planks. Then he had painted it all bright red, with white lines intended to look like bricks. The *pièce de résistance* was a tatty piece of dirty white bobble-fringing roughly tacked along the supporting bressummer beam.

"Quel affreux!" ("What a fright!") pronounced my builder Monsieur Doumesche, on seeing it later that year. Restoring this magnificent fireplace and re-routing the flue was sixth on the list. A hardboard partition around the top of the stairs blocked light from the stairwell. That would have to go too, as would the layers of carpet, lino and hardboard covering what looked like some fine chestnut floorboards. On the same floor is the main bedroom, nicely proportioned with windows at either end. The walls were covered with brown printed hessian, stapled every half-inch onto battens, as the girls painfully

discovered later, when they laboriously removed every single staple with pliers.

A loft-ladder set into the *lambris* (wood-cladding) ceiling led to the roof space. This *grenier*, floored with ancient planks, had reasonable headroom under the main joists, at least for those under 5ft 5ins! Rough wooden strips lined the roof for insulation and the area was lit by two tiny metal-framed skylights. It also had woodworm, or rather holes that no ordinary English woodworm could have made. My little fingertip fitted into them, but we were assured that these beetles did no serious harm, as they only penetrated into the softwood and then tunnelled sideways along the beams. Ripping off the outer strips from the holes exposed totally dry wood-dust, but the inside of the beams appeared solid and hard. As nobody expects to have a survey done in France, we had to take the builder's word that the house was reasonably sound, the exterior cracks were superficial and the beams wouldn't collapse in spite of the rampant woodworm. I was reminded while writing this of Julian Barnes' "A History of the World in 10½ Chapters", where the first part of the story is recounted by one of seven stowaways on Noah's Ark. It is not until the end of the chapter that he declares himself to be one of the few animals specifically *not* chosen to accompany Noah... a woodworm! Most of the enormous loft space was littered with the old couple's abandoned debris, which included a huge plain and ugly bed, a mattress, personal papers, fibreglass insulation still in its wrapping, clothes, Monsieur Coruble's Second World War military uniform and his fishing medals, chairs, and books, including a fascinating volume of photos from the First World War.

Back outside, we climbed the wide uneven stone steps at the side of the house, which led to the former main front door still emblazoned with a religious metal plaque. The top step, or rather the 6ft square area under the porch roof, seemed hollow. Investigating the dusty cobwebbed space beneath, we discovered that there was nothing at all in the wood store holding up this step. Above, a red tiled roof was barely supported by its rotten beams. But after re-roofing and positioning concrete supports under the step, this side porch made an excellent little store for garden chairs and the barbecue. Continuing round the path at the side of the house we found a big filthy storeroom full of smelly decaying potatoes, preserving jars, empty paint tins, sad old chairs, shredded grey net curtains hanging randomly from a few hooks and enormous spiders' webs draped everywhere. This space had potential for development, but on first sight appeared an impossibly daunting task. Beyond this lean-to, a narrow path led to a well fed by a spring, which seemed to be of little use, though we found out later who was now using it. Our next door neighbour has a luxuriant vegetable garden! Tiny, extremely randomly-laid stone steps led up the side of a retaining wall to an upper level of the garden, which should have been grassed, but nurtured a varied collection of vigorous weeds. Several large fir trees blocked the view down the valley from a small concrete terrace with a solid table in the middle, made of concrete and decorated with a crazy patchwork of broken tiles. Over this was a vine-draped, perilously leaning pergola. The front garden was also overgrown, with iris, primulas and hundreds of lily of the valley each side of a crazy-paved path. Several interesting trees and shrubs, including a fine flowering magnolia, buddleia, syringa, rhododendron, vast hydrangeas and many hibiscuses were flourishing. At the entrance, a metal-mesh gate spanned two sturdy stone and brick gateposts.

The house is approached up a short spur from a back road, which leads up the steep, tree-clad hillside – 'the up and over road' as we nicknamed it. From this often damp and mossy road glimpses of the River Dordogne, bright blue in the sunshine, are occasionally visible when the trees are not too full of leaf. The little village where our home is situated nestles on a small, gently rising plain where strawberries and walnuts are grown. The early strawberries are cultivated in polytunnels, and appear in the shops at Easter, and the last ones are picked in November. It's a foodies' paradise!

We walked into the village down a little track just wide enough for a horse and cart, which was the main road a century ago, past our neighbour's chicken run below the house and a large barn on our right. Ancient stone houses covered with *crêpi*, others seemingly splitting in two with great vertical cracks rending their walls, lined the narrow track running down a gentle slope into the main street. Glancing into small barns and storerooms we discovered a flock of about seven sheep huddling together in the dark recesses of an undercroft to one of the old houses. Hunting dogs, penned behind high fences, barked out a greeting or a warning – we didn't intend to find out which. Then we explored the walled graveyard, full of huge stone tombs. Many were decorated with plastic flowers or faded bouquets made of tiny glass beads, though some were clearly still lovingly attended by the family, with fresh flowers carefully arranged. Small plaques of metal or china showed photos of the departed, and some displayed touching messages: 'From a loving nephew' or, 'Thinking of my dearest uncle for ever'. Thankfully it is not full of the peculiar glass greenhouses, designed to protect the stone family vaults from the weather, which one sees looming over churchyard walls all over France. Outside the gates is a small, neatly-kept war memorial to the local dead of both World Wars. Such a tiny community to lose so many sons.

Next to the churchyard is the ancient Romanesque village church, with its rounded porch and simple single nave construction. Modern glass in rather garish colours has been put in all the church windows, as in many other churches around the district. One wonders if they originally had plain glass, or whether the stained glass was smashed during the Wars of Religion. Protestantism swept over much of this area, though it is now firmly Catholic. I tried the harmonium, but it only produced a few wheezy, out-of-tune notes. All the services must be unaccompanied. The altar and its surrounding carving are elaborate and colourful, with the 'All seeing eye' in a triangle,

The ancient Romanesque village church

representing the Holy Trinity at the apex of the design. Turning round, one can see spindly wooden stairs rising to a precarious-looking gallery. It seems unlikely that it is used nowadays (apart from the danger it might pose) as the village is small, and few attend church regularly. Funerals, remembrance services for war dead, occasional weddings and festivals draw the biggest congregations. The rough wooden floor sounded hollow, though there was no obvious access to a vault or crypt. A tunnel, we were told later, runs from the church, under the road to an apparently ordinary old house on the other side. This house has a small turret housing a spiral staircase and a beautiful Renaissance doorway, only visible from a short drive at one side. And in the back garden is a pepper-pot roofed *pigeonnier*, where pigeons would have been kept for winter meat not so long ago. It is rumoured that this house belonged to the family of Marguerite of Valois, who married Henry IV of France in 1572. Certainly some of its architectural details tie up with this date.

On the other side of the church a small well-tended garden with benches, grass, shrubs and a gravel *boules* pitch, has been created for the village. This made me think again of my father, who had always been so fond of France and its way of life. After my mother's death he married a charming French lady, about twelve years younger than he was. They sporadically talked about moving to France, a move I enthusiastically encouraged. But nothing came of it. I often have an image of what his life might have been like, had they taken the plunge. As a keen and talented chess and snooker player, and a reasonably good French speaker, he would have fitted so easily into the sociable life old men lead in the South of France. I could envisage him sitting around in a village square, nattering with his mates, drinking moderately, watching the young girls passing by and enjoying his chess games. Instead, he lived till the age of 92, in London, reluctantly going out, and with most of his friends long dead.

We walked on, past the newly-restored Mairie, part of which

was formerly the village school. Next door we found the *boulangerie*, brightly adorned with tidy pots of flowering plants that Madame Gravier constantly cosseted, trimming off dead flowers and sweeping the fallen leaves. She created a wonderfully colourful little corner, with a round metal table and chairs outside the shop, where her two spoilt cats, one ginger, the other a soft tabby, held court. Occasionally the naughty ginger cat leapt up onto the serving counter, but no one seemed to mind. *Baguettes* and the local coarse round *tourtes* were made fresh every day by Monsieur Gravier, who drove his old van full of aromatic loaves to outlying hamlets each day. The privilege of having a local baker fulfilled my prime request. I walked down through the village, as I had always seen myself doing, every morning for my breakfast bread, and to share a social chat about the weather or the progress with our house with the neighbours. Monsieur Gravier has now retired and the pleasure of the walk, the chats and the appetising hot bread smells drifting up the street, are sadly no more.

Continuing past a steaming heap of manure, with chickens scratching for worms among the rotting straw, we passed more old houses on what had been the continuation of the main through-road. Turning right at a tiny crossroads, we walked between old barns with strangely carved heads set into the stonework above the patched and worn doorways, eventually coming to a stop on the remains of an old bridge. It was replaced in the 1930s by a new, but not ungraceful, reinforced concrete bridge, about 50 yards upstream. The river is wide and shallow at this point, with a miniature sandy beach where canoes can be put into the water and beyond the new bridge is a gravelly shoal, popular with wader-clad fishermen hoping for a good catch of trout.

Returning to the crossing we followed the constricted ancient road and turned again to walk onto the new bridge. On the other side of the river the hills rise almost vertically. Reddish rocks, clearly showing two rectangular holes, which were probably lookout points used during the last war, punctuate the lush growth of chestnut and oak trees. Hundreds of acacia trees, their white pendulous flowers a magnet for honeybees, hung over the river bank. In the distance we could just see a bend where the water is shallow enough to create the rapids we had heard from the house. Returning along the main road we passed two old-fashioned bars, a post office and a workshop where Monsieur Feldis made and sold furniture and kitchens. Many of the houses were adorned with flower-filled window boxes and pots, making what is quite a plain main street colourful and welcoming. A few residents greeted us with a courteous *"Bonjour"*. We were, by now, quite sure that we were making the right choice.

Back at our freezing rented house, huddled round the log fire, we mulled over the problems and possibilities of turning a one-bedroom house into a four-bedroomed one. The list of improvements seemed endless. It needed a new window in the kitchen, the sink replaced and some kitchen storage units built. We would have to replace the bathroom window, and, eventually those in the lean-to, and knock through from the lobby to the lean-to, making steps up through the wall and floor, as it is on a different level to the rest of the house. Then we wanted to install French windows front and back to this room, repoint the stone walls, cover the concrete floor with terracotta tiles and re-align the roof, as its pitch was too shallow. In the living-room we needed to resite the boiler flue to one side, cover it with *crêpi* and make a small chimney for it, then restore the fireplace. I also planned to have window seats with hinged lids for storage in all the living room window embrasures. At the top of the stairs we would remove the hardboard partition and install some banisters, and replace the existing sloping banisters to match. To gain sensible access to the loft we needed to knock through the wall at the top of the stairs and install a new staircase to the roof-space, panelling the bedroom side with woodstrips, like the ceiling. The roof-space could be divided into two bedrooms with new sockets and lighting installed, and the skylights replaced with Velux windows. The ceiling in the loft needed insulated plasterboard set between each of the rafters. Of course there was that hideous glass porch to remove and the oil store to rebuild. After we had considered the practical, structural improvements necessary to make a sensible home without being too 'arty-farty', we then started on decorative schemes and furnishing ideas.

"Our room will be green and yellow," declared Lulu, taking a close personal interest in the whole project.

Having got the business of the trip out of the way we allowed ourselves a few days of proper holiday. One scorching day we ate wonderful savoury *crêpes* followed by enormous ice creams drenched in liqueurs and heaped with *crême chantilly*, at a delightful vine-clad *crêperie* at the end of the Quai des Gabariers, by the bridge in Argentat, a few miles upstream. The town was a great centre in the not- too-distant past, where the *gabariers* would make their simple flat-bottomed boats, *gabares*, for transporting oak for wine barrels downstream to Bordeaux. People say that the boats were dragged back upstream, roped to horses who walked along the towpath. Others say that the *gabares* were broken up and sold at the end of their journey, as the river is too fast and full of rapids for a return trip. Money from the sale of the barrel-wood or the sale of the demolished boats was then used to buy a donkey or mule on which the *gabarier* would return home. Certainly, the quality of the houses flanking the river here is far superior to many along the river, so I guess that there was much money to be made in timber (or donkeys).

On returning to England, we just had to wait for the completion to be finalised by Anne, the *notaire*, and the owner. But things were not to prove as simple as they had seemed in France.

Chapter 5

SLAVING OVER A COLD SINK

In May I returned to the cottage we had rented at Easter. So sure was I that the sale would go ahead, that I took down three old bikes and several boxes full of bits and pieces to leave at the house, for when the girls and I came back in the summer. From our notes, and from memory, I had compiled the extensive list of necessary improvements and structural repairs, which I struggled to translate into French. Since I had not studied French beyond O Level and had used my limited knowledge of the language only rarely afterwards, I had some difficulty, particularly with the words for hardboard, lino, breeze blocks, power points and such-like. I typed out this list, room by room. Laid out this way it now seemed quite a formidable project.

The *notaire*'s secretary recommended me to Monsieur

Doumesche, a *maçon*, basically a builder who specialises in working with stone. He was charmingly old-fashioned, full of pleasant courtesy, though he spoke so fast, and with an incomprehensible rural accent, that I was lucky if I understood one word in ten. In fact, I found that the only way I could be sure I would get what I wanted was to begin talking first. I would describe what needed to be done, give him a plan or sketch and a written description and then hope for the best, as I was never quite sure I had understood his comments and additions to my ideas. However, he seemed to gather what I wanted and he seemed interested in doing the job. My most difficult request was concerning the fireplace. I couldn't find the specific word for flue, in French, as opposed to a chimney, nor could I discover the word for a hearth. I therefore had to ask that the chimney (flue for the boiler) should be removed from the chimney and a new chimney (flue) placed to the side of the old chimney and the floor of the chimney (hearth) be repaired. Remarkably, he understood it all and did the work most expertly. It now looks like it probably did before Monsieur Coruble started his 'improvements'. After a few dozen log fires the back wall was nicely blackened as if it had been untouched for a hundred years and recently I found a nice cast iron French fireback in an English antique fair to prop against the back wall.

I asked Monsieur Doumesche to suggest the other workmen we would need, an electrician, plumber, plasterer and carpenter – people he knew and would be happy to work with. On returning home after this trip I wrote to each of his friends and made appointments to meet them at the house in July. Each one turned up on the right day at the right time. Could you expect, or achieve that in England? Each then received my poorly translated list of work to be done, with their contribution highlighted, and each was told, with some amused reactions, that Monsieur Doumesche was 'Boss' and would call on them as and when he needed them. The telephone company also sent their engineers on the day I had requested, though in fact they told me they had come the previous day, as they were just passing and thought they could connect me then, but since I wasn't there, they returned as arranged. This too seemed remarkable to us, used to delays of weeks, if not months before a phone can be installed in England.

Convinced that our purchase would go ahead, I visited Monsieur Feldis, the local kitchen fitter, and asked him to come to the house as I needed new units, a sink and a splashback. "I'll just change my shoes," he said, and came immediately, notebook and measure in hand. I ordered a simple kitchen in pine (not being able to afford the superior oak), with a honey-coloured double sink, matching tiles and unusual twisted metal handles. I asked for it all to be made and fitted by the summer, when the girls and I intended to come back to start decorating the areas which were not going to be affected by building work. The kitchen design incorporated a tall cupboard for china and food storage, which neatly covered an unusual, inconvenient, but presumably necessary, internal buttress. The cupboard shelves reduce in depth towards the bottom, but this is not obvious from the outside. At a large furniture shop in Brive I bought a cheap gas cooker that uses bottled gas, and left it in the house so that the kitchen units could be planned around it. It serves its purpose, as the oven is either hot or very hot! Friends in the area say that their cookers seem to be just as inefficient, even if they have cost a lot more. Maybe it's the bottled gas.

Shortly after getting back to England the first major hiccup occurred. Monsieur Coruble, the owner, died! Not only could he not sign any papers, but in his will, instead of leaving the property to his daughter, with whom we had been negotiating, he left it to two nephews, one of whom was simple-minded and likely to be slow about making any decisions. The daughter, however, was determined that the sale would go ahead. Letters and phone calls went to and fro for about three weeks before we learnt that both nephews were willing to sell. Now all the papers had to be redrawn and signed again, and the probate proved. None of these legal procedures was simple and negotiations dragged. Eventually the daughter gave us permission to move in during July, even though we still did not legally own the house by then. Tony was appalled. As a lawyer, he knew we had no rights at all, and could probably be sued for causing damage to the house if we did any structural work. Also we could lose any belongings we had left there, including the planned kitchen, if the owners reneged on the deal.

During the few months between my visits I had not been idle. I had been searching out bargains and decorative treasures with which to furnish our house. Solid wooden-framed armchairs (flat-packed) came from The Reject Shop. The cushions were boringly covered in a pale beige check, so I recovered them with navy fabric found for £1 a yard in a local market. However, putting the frames together was not as simple as it should have been, as the canvas-covered bases were about an inch too short. I had to undo all the screws with which the canvas was attached and reposition them correctly. My hands were blistered and sore from wielding the screwdriver for so many hours. If only I'd thought to buy an electric screwdriver.

A Swedish company supplied a cornflower blue convertible sofa bed, also for the living room. At least this came in larger, ready-made sections. An unwanted bookcase in pine was sawn in half across the middle to create two storage units, one of which now houses the TV and video, and the other displays my books about France. Another old bookcase from our English home holds quantities of local maps and guidebooks. Many hardback novels, by well-known writers such as Hemingway and Laurie Lee, which I am sure many visitors have always intended to read, were chosen from my own collection or bought from charity shops.

The fabric from which I made curtains, window seat covers and some cushions, was another excellent bargain. I saw the material with its pretty blues, mauves and pinks, with an abstract design, not unlike a Matisse painting, and asked the assistant whether the sample in the book was meant to be the same colourway as that on a roll they had on display. She replied that it should have been, but was slightly different as the roll was 'seconds' and was therefore half-price. "I'll take the lot," I said, pipping to the post someone else who had appeared interested.

Still ridiculously confident that everything would be sorted out to our satisfaction, Pippa, Lulu and I returned in the July, to find no kitchen units, no sink, nothing done and the floor awash. Horrified, I ran down the road to find Monsieur Feldis to discover why the work hadn't been done. His measured reply was that the main water pipe was leaking. He had removed the old sink and cupboard and found the floor too wet to install the new units, which he assured me were very nearly ready. Why he had not called the water authority himself I cannot imagine. After a few frantic phone calls I discovered who I needed to contact and their engineer cheerfully spent much of the next day fixing the leak and replacing the meter. None of the joints matched those he had brought and it took considerable skill to remake all the sections.

A week later we still had no hot water as the boiler refused to work, and we still had no sink, so we had to wash up in the hand basin and shower in cold water. It was a good thing that the weather was hot (so hot in fact that the girls did some of the decorating and cleaning in their swimming costumes), so cold showers weren't such a bad thing. Monsieur Feldis has since retired from his furniture making, just a few years after building an enormous, and now redundant showroom on the main road, but his legacy in my kitchen was exactly as I'd planned.

For the first few days that hot July, the girls and I lived at a simple *auberge* nearby, where lorry drivers stayed overnight or stopped to eat amply and amazingly cheaply. It is noticeable all over France that workmen take a long lunch break in order to eat well and inexpensively at the many Relais Routiers along the main roads. The French appear to demand, and get, good quality meals, whoever and wherever they are. This attitude is in vivid contrast with most average English workmen who

41

seem satisfied with a sandwich or a burger and a thermos of tea. Visiting the house each day from the *auberge*, we worked like slaves, wearing grooves in the road to the local hypermarket and cheap furniture stores. 'Local' in this area means 25 miles away! We acquired a fridge and beds, all of which were transported in – or on – our trusty Renault 25, as had the other furniture I had brought from England. The loaders who attempted to help us with the beds realised that we three women were quite capable, indeed somewhat faster and neater at lashing large bits of furniture onto our car, and stood around applauding our expertise.

Monsieur Doumesche arrived one day saying that he had time to do one job, so what would we like him to do. "The porch!" we all chorused. Immediately he set about demolishing the despised carbuncle. As soon as the water was turned on we moved into the house, camping in the living room, where we assembled three of our beds. Pippa couldn't bear to live with the red-painted sink alcove, and roughly painted it white. She also developed a strong aversion to the false brick interior of the fireplace and quickly covered that in white paint too. More dramatically, she decided one day to demolish the living room partition, which she attacked with a hammer and her bare hands. Together we destroyed the ghastly dining room dresser, retaining the marble tops for use as a garden table.

Our primary task was to clear the main rooms and loft of years of accumulated junk, though we found some treasures among the dross. We kept the tatty dining table, whose warped leaves, totally devoid of all varnish, I later unearthed in the lean-to storeroom. It is not a fine piece of furniture, and an oil-cloth had been left, clinging stubbornly to the remains of the polish on the tabletop. However, with a new wipeable red checked cloth permanently left on, the leaves repaired and screwed firmly to the table, it is eminently functional. Several rush-seated chairs, their legs slightly mouse-chewed, which we found in the loft, are now usefully employed around the bedrooms. An old-fashioned metal-legged bedside table only required a round MDF top nailed onto it to make a pretty lamp table, when disguised with a floor-length navy cloth with a white lace-edged Victorian tea tablecloth placed over it. A rusting metal cube, whose original purpose I cannot imagine, was painted dark green, to find a new use as a garden table, topped with the reserved marble slab. I'm sure we could have found a use for more of the rubbish, both from the storeroom and the loft, had we had the forethought.

We began to tackle the disgusting storeroom at the back of the house. I was terrified of the possibility that rats were living there and made the girls stand well back while I toppled the old doors, balanced against the walls, which held back the stinking heap of old potatoes. I was heartily relieved to see no rats jumping out, but didn't have the courage to continue the formidable task of clearing the whole rotting mess. Again, Monsieur Doumesche came to the rescue and shovelled it all away before beginning this room's transformation. Most of the junk from the roof-space was bundled up, dragged down the loft-ladder hole, thrown down the outside steps onto the paving and humped down the path to be left outside our gate (much to the disapproval of our neighbour's dour son), to await disposal by the kind Monsieur Doumesche.

In the main bedroom the girls bravely tackled the depressing painted hessian, prising out every staple and ripping down the fabric. The battens were far too firmly attached to remove, so they were left in place and painted over. When that was accomplished they painted the walls white and we all decamped to the bedroom and started on the living room. My first job was to repair the windowsills and other woodwork and then paint the windows and doors. One day Monsieur Farge, the plumber, arrived to try to get the boiler fixed (having replaced one £100 item only to discover that it still didn't work) and found the girls busy downstairs. He said that he presumed I was having a siesta, so wouldn't disturb me. The girls laughed at the idea of having time to rest and directed him up to the living room, where I was painting the window frames a beautiful lilac blue.

"Ah, la vie en bleu," he declared, and we both laughed, as I recognised his reference to *"La Vie en Rose,"* a lovely Edith Piaf classic. His subtle humour demonstrated another remarkable difference between the average English workman and a French one. But in spite of his pleasant demeanour it wasn't until we had left that he finally got the boiler going! However, he did convert the valves on the cooker, so that we could use bottled, rather than natural gas. All went well until I tried to light the oven, which ignited with a whoosh and a sheet of flame shot across my feet and the floor. Thank goodness my reactions were fast enough to turn the switch off before anything caught fire. I was, amazingly, quite unhurt and after yet another visit, Monsieur Farge fitted the oven valve correctly so we could at last have hot meals. Salads had got rather boring.

Lulu wanted to paint the shutters, whose pins easily slid off their simple hinges so that they could be worked on flat, though they were heavy to lift. It was the green paint that had been used by Monsieur Coruble on the shutters and gates, together with the dark green and (formerly white, now grubby grey) tiled floor in the kitchen, which defined our choice of name for the house. The paintwork and floor, and the generally green and lush nature of the scenery helped us to name it 'La Folie Verte'. We had considered 'Chanterelle,' a wild mushroom, as an alternative, because the idea of having a French house had grown like a mushroom, but it was also a play on the words *'chant'* (sing) and *'elle'* (she), which would have neatly described my principal hobby and me. But the idea of a 'folly', as a foolish, purposeless structure seemed more appropriate. It had been my mad idea to buy a house in the first place, and I subsequently discovered that *'folie'* in eighteenth century France actually meant 'a country house for recreation'. So 'La Folie Verte ' it was.

Having done what improvements we could, the girls and I reluctantly closed the house for the summer and left. In the Autumn I returned with Tony, for his first view of 'La Folie

Verte'. Seeing it in an almost raw state, he was unsure that my vision of a charming, relaxing holiday home was what was facing him. I tried to convince him of the wisdom of our choice and the possibilities the house would offer in the future. So he buckled to, and together we worked hard, getting the garden into some sort of shape, hacking down the overgrown meadow that was supposed to be a lawn and pruning the shrubs hard, removing several years of rampant growth. After a week of determined digging and chopping it all looked a lot more like a garden. We couldn't tackle much in the house at this stage since most of the structural work had to be done by professional builders, so we bravely left the house in their hands for the winter, wondering what we would find in the Spring.

Chapter 6

CHICKENS, PARROTS AND PLANTS

Remarkably, most of what we had requested had been done, and done beautifully. The banisters beside the stairs in the kitchen were upright, no longer inducing seasickness. The lobby beyond the kitchen had new steps leading up to a transformed storeroom. This, we now realised was on a very much higher level than had appeared, and Monsieur Doumesche had obviously had an enormous job removing stones from the exterior wall, which had been built against the higher ground. He then had to tunnel up through this ground, or dig down through the old concrete floor, and after all this work had created a neat set of steps without taking up too much of the floor space. He had scraped out the crumbling mortar and repointed the exposed stones of the walls. The roof of the storeroom was realigned and re-roofed and French doors replaced the old solid ones. My vision was becoming a reality.

In the living room the fireplace had been stripped of painted plaster, the bressummer beam exposed and the newly-exposed stone wall repointed. The floor of the hearth was repaired and the new flue hidden behind a grey *crêpi* wall to one side, where it is not at all noticeable. Wooden banisters replaced the hardboard cupboard which Pippa had so enthusiastically demolished. A fine new staircase led to the upper floor where two bedrooms had been created out of the filthy loft, their plasterboard ceilings carefully fitted between the curvaceous beams. What really impressed me a great deal was the thoughtfulness of the builders and carpenters. They had worked out how to solve many problems, like the design of the turn of the stairs so that your head does not hit the steeply sloping roof as you reach the little landing. There was lighting in the loft, on the stairs and in the old storeroom – now known as the Garden Room – and sockets had been installed where they were needed. The water was hot. The radiators worked.

We assembled more flat-pack furniture (still foolishly without buying that much-needed electric screwdriver), ending up with several bedside chests and small coffee tables, a chest of drawers for each bedroom, and a rocking chair. I put up curtain tracks and tiebacks, using my trusty electric drill for every hole as the walls are solid as concrete. My expertise with drills dates back to my teenage years when, on asking my brother for help with a shelf, I was told to get wood, brackets, screws, etc. He then gave me his drill, quickly showed me how to use it and left me to my own devices. I learnt! I had finished making the curtains for the living room and main bedroom, and brought the bedspreads I had also made during the winter. It seemed like a home, but we were not yet finished with our improvement schedule.

We approached the neighbours who owned the chicken run adjoining our village-facing wall, to ask if they would allow us to put in a kitchen window, which would then overlook their chickens. Their answer was "No," but they immediately suggested that we could buy half of the land, with seven cherry trees, at the price they had agreed some years ago with the now deceased Monsieur Coruble. They claimed that he had also wanted to extend his land, so that the house could stand more or less within its own ground (though the back wall still abuts the lush vegetable plot I mentioned before). They offered to put up a fence and to call the *géomètre*, a land surveyor, whom the law demands must measure and assign new numbers to any divided parcels of land for the records. We thought the price rather high at the time, but agreed to their full demands. It has improved the amenities enormously. Not only did the purchase allow us to put in the window (for which we forgot to apply for planning permission), but also gave us space to park two cars and plant some new trees, including a very thriving walnut, after the cherry trees had sadly died. I don't think the former owner put a hex on them, as his died too! It seemed to be a local disease, which only affected cherries. We have now built a swimming pool in part of this area, which would not have been possible in the upper garden.

Monsieur Doumesche was consulted about the kitchen window, which needed a large hole excavated from the stone walls. After taking measurements he declared: "What have we here, a fortress?" The walls are at least three feet thick so he must have removed a vast heap of stones, as well as hoisting several concrete lintels into place. Outside he constructed the window with large cut stones, similar to those surrounding the upstairs window, at little more than the cost of rough stonework. Just imagine what that would have cost in England! When he had finished the window looked as if it had always been there, which is why I think no one bothered us about the planning permission.

The carpenter replaced several old unmatching and rotten windows in the Garden Room with solid made-to-measure ones of wood, and in the same room he installed a French door overlooking the village. The Garden Room also acquired another name, the 'Parrot Room', after a large balsa wood parrot and snake sculpture which Pippa had brought back for me from Ecuador. Parrots also appear in the pictures on the walls and on a huge Indian 'Tree of Life' bedspread, which I bought in a charity shop in Cambridge to cover a rough-plastered wall which has a long, deep, apparently unimportant crack in it! Monsieur Farge laid inexpensive terracotta tiles on the floor and the steps from the lobby, and Monsieur Doumesche built some stone-faced concrete steps leading down from the French door of the Parrot Room to the lower garden. This room has been transformed into one of the nicest in the house, peaceful and secluded. I chose bright lime green striped curtains, jungle print cushions, a plain rug and furnished it with cane chairs and small chests, a navy sofa-bed and an old pine wardrobe and cupboard. A keen DIY friend subsequently put up navy blinds for me, as this is the room I like to sleep in during the summer. It is cool and private, and has the best view of the village from its tiny terrace, just big enough for a table and one chair at the top of the steps. All this out of that incredibly revolting storeroom we had first seen. It certainly had needed imagination.

Monsieur Doumesche then cut a hole through the wall which divided the two bits of the garden and later hung a pretty wrought iron gate with a curved top to link the two ends of the wall which were of different heights. Its scrolls were designed by me to echo a small balustrade, also of wrought iron, which protects the set of narrow, uneven steps joining the lower to the upper levels of the garden. I had had the heavy gate made in England and, as usual with all the stuff I had brought down, it was transported on the roof of the long-suffering Renault.

Next to the nasty porch (now no more) was the great oil tank in its perfunctory shelter. I redesigned this as a *crêpi*-covered lean-to building, roofed with old tiles to match the side porch. This roof, in my drawing, extended over the French doors to the kitchen and was supported by a simple hand-

49

carved oak brace. I planned to reuse the old doors from the garden room at the side of the new oil store, and put in a small offset window to the front to break up its plain wall. The plans were submitted through the Mairie in the village and I awaited their approval. This was denied! Since the existing structure was unsound and positively ruined the front and side aspects of the house, I made an appointment with the *département*'s planning architect to find out what to do. He initially said that I couldn't do anything as we were in a conservation area, but when I showed him photos of the existing monstrosity, he admitted that it didn't improve the look of the house. I suggested that if he didn't like my plans, he should draw up a design he would approve of and perhaps we could apply again for planning permission with those. Surprisingly he was not offended by my suggestion and decided that it must be in stone, even though the front wall above the lean-to had been mostly covered with crêpi. Then he insisted that the window was placed centrally and that no porch should be added. I reluctantly agreed to his plans – though I felt he was wrong – and sent them to Monsieur Doumesche. A year later, when he was ready to start work, he came to discuss the proposed building work.

"Now, where was the end of the building?" he asked, and then exclaimed, "Oh, yes, here" as he indicated a pencil mark he had made on the wall 18 months or so before. Then he said something about the position of the window. I assured him that I had sent him the plans, but he claimed to have lost them!

"The window should be offset. It will look better," he said, "and what about the porch, to here I think…"

I told him that we had been told to place the window centrally, and not to build a porch at all. "Oh, you've got to have a porch," he insisted. "It will protect the door from the rain."

He built the oil store beautifully, just like my original plans; the window is offset and a practical and attractive porch protects the front door, though the walls are in stone, as we had been instructed. No one from the Council ever came to see it and the front elevation of the house is improved immensely. The new addition, like the kitchen window, looks as if it has been there for years.

After a storm brought down a small tree on a corner of the roof, and some of the slates crashed down onto the terrace, we were advised to replace the roof, an expensive exercise, though not as expensive as it might have been. The roofing contractor gave us a fixed price in French francs to do the job, saying that he would use as many of the old shell-shaped slates as he could salvage and find others to match if necessary. He said he would do the work during the winter. However, we arrived in Spring to find the roof as before. Due to illness the work was not done until two years later, by which time the franc had gone down in value, so our roof was about £1000 cheaper than we had expected.

The temperamental old boiler eventually wore out, too, and replacing this cost a lot of money. Considering that it only feeds the kitchen sink, two basins, a shower or bath and four radiators, its vast size seems grossly disproportionate. It looks big enough to heat a school, but it works on a different system to most English ones, having no storage tanks. At least it's superbly efficient and out of sight in its little room off the kitchen.

Quite recently a basin and loo were installed between the two rooms in the loft. It was my intention to do this when we could afford it, and the cost was so reasonable that I wish we had done it years before. The larger room has lost three feet but still appears quite big enough for two. A minor problem occurred when I tried to put up a light fitting in the little landing outside the new loo, between the bedrooms. The walls were constructed of metal framing with plasterboard infill, rather than the stud partitioning I am used to. There was a wire, with a bare bulb in a plain holder sticking out of the wall. I attempted to drill holes to fix up an unusual flower and leaf wall-light I had bought especially for this wall, but there was nothing solid to drill into. Having discovered this the hard way

– I now had a 3in hole in the plasterboard – I found an old plank of wood, drilled a hole in it for the projecting wires, and wedged it between a joist and a horizontal beam. I could now attach the light-fitting to the plank, which looks like it is part of the original structure of the roof. Creating the new loo also enabled a storage cupboard for blankets and pillows to be made under the eaves, though this has proved to be the most popular place in the house for mice to congregate. Sometimes they eat their way through a large bowl of poison-tainted grain in one day and come back for more the next, as if they are thriving on it.

Furniture for Folie was gathered from many obvious and other less obvious sources. I had such a lot of fun going to antiques fairs and markets and searching for bargains everywhere I went. The main bedroom curtains and bedspread, in bright turquoise raw silk, had been a gift from a former client and had already done service in her house in London and then in one of our bedrooms in England. In fact I had remade them once already and created the bedcover from one of the enormous lengths of material. A huge pine wardrobe, which demounted into four sections, together with a chest with three drawers, was bought from a friend who didn't need them any more as she was moving. A very pretty pine washstand came from another friend whose second husband hated pine, so I took that off her hands for a modest price. On top of this I placed a swing mirror, found in an auction, which I had stripped and polished. The wrought iron light-fitting cost £10. It was dirty and black when I found it, but is now painted soft turquoise and coral, to go with a striped durrie and a Victorian jug and washbasin which has a flower and ribbon pattern. The design on the china is similar to a stencilled frieze, which I worked on in my rare free hours over the next few years. Some of the pictures are slightly saucy prints in typical French fashion. I saw some of these in an exhibition about French Women in Art in England, and immediately thought I would like to collect them. The very next week I found one at an antiques fair in Hampton Court, and then took at least another five years before finding another. A tiny pine wall-hung cupboard, where I store a sewing kit, supports a pair of artist's model figures. It has become a tradition for Pippa or I to leave them in a new pose each time we go. Most often they are left as a pair of dancers doing ballet, or Spanish Flamenco. It's a little private message to each other.

For the living room I bought a large cream flokati rug for half-price in Brighton, and other durries for use on the floor or the walls. I cut foam, bought in Kingston market, for the window seat cushions and covered them with some of the curtain material. Brass trays, candlesticks, including a swivelling double one which must have been removed from a piano, and other decorative metal items, were purchased on a hurried visit to the antiques market in Yeovil, when I was meant to be teaching art to adults at a Field Studies Centre in North Somerset. The redundant sink unit now displays a large arrangement of silk flowers. Fresh ones would be lovely, but just not practical. Another alcove houses an old embroiderer's oil lamp, its modest light magnified by the convex mirror behind it. Pippa had romantically envisaged herself sitting in a rocking chair in the kitchen podding peas or preparing beans (too many American films!), so we bought one (which she put together) in cane and bentwood. Unfortunately we couldn't find room for it in the kitchen, so it was added to the armchairs in the living room. A discreet modern metal and glass-topped table incredibly has survived the visits of paying guests.

I bought a TV and video and took down many good films, which are extremely popular with guests on wet days in, or to keep youngsters amused while food is being prepared. I also flop in front of the video, with my after-dinner coffee and a chocolate, or a glass of something nice, when I am alone at the house. Charity shops are occasionally a cheap source for films I haven't seen before, otherwise I find ex-rental videos or record them from the television at home. The list of films I want to see gets shorter as I catch up with several each time I

53

go down. After Pippa had finished an MBA course at a college near Versailles, some time after we had acquired 'Folie', I inherited her already second-hand French TV, which she had used to help improve her language skills. I must admit that I don't watch it as often as I should. My French too, could do with a lot of improvement. But I do sometimes catch up on the news and weather. The bookcases are now full up, the games and puzzles shelf groaning under Scrabble, Backgammon, Othello and the like, and there is a guitar and an electric keyboard for the odd moments when I have time to do some practice, which doesn't happen often.

Two Italian gilded plaster *torchères*, bought in Surrey, were cleverly converted by another friend into chandeliers for the living room and kitchen. It may seem excessively grand to hang a chandelier in the kitchen, but it works, as does the apparently clashing colour scheme. The walls are yellow, the provençal fabric for the curtain mainly red, with some green and yellow, and the chairs are dark green stained wood. I indulge my taste for pretty, bright provençal materials and put a fabric cloth over the red oilcloth-covered table when I am in residence. In Brive I bought a cupboard and a set of shelves, which, placed one above the other, look like a dresser. I have filled these shelves with hand-painted and sponge-printed china, some chipped and cracked, so they are just for decoration, not for use. And it looks good. More china plates, Greek rugs and Thai fabrics, useful baskets, two wrought iron brackets in the form of bunches of grapes (for hats), *pâté* dishes in the shape of birds and a rabbit, green pewter-lidded coffee pots and a breadboard with 'Give us this day our daily bread' carved into the border in French add to the rustic and friendly appeal of the most used room of the house. All this decorative clutter helps to make it feel like a home. Our regular summer companions always arrive with smiles and sighs of pleasure as they exclaim each time, "Ah, home!"

For the girls' room I hunted high and low for the perfect green and yellow material (as demanded by Lulu), to make into bedspreads, eventually tracking down a fabric with a bold tulip design. Amazingly I found a picture in a car boot sale that went with the tulips exactly. Ikea provided a bright yellow rag rug, and another striped flat-weave rug completed the room. The second little room, which delights young children, is L-shaped, as it is built around the new staircase. Some of the walls are a strong sky blue, some white. White bedspreads and two lovely Romanian durries with flowers woven onto a turquiose background complete this charming hideaway. As with many of my acquisitions, there is a strange story to account for these rugs. Someone who had seen an advertise-ment for my Interior Design services in a local magazine, phoned me. She asked if I would like to buy some rugs for my clients. I replied that I never bought 'on spec', as one couldn't be sure of reselling, so I didn't keep any stock and I didn't need any rugs myself. Suffice it to say that she was very persuasive and I ended up buying five. I now wish I had taken the lot. They were incredibly cheap. Her husband had brought them back in the lorry in which he had transported a load of sugar to Romania, when there were desperate shortages after the fall of Ceaucescu. Two beautiful blue rugs now grace my studio in England and Vicky had the fifth one for her flat. Though adults sometimes use these roof rooms, there is limited headroom under the tie beams, so children find it a perfect haven. There is a shelf of children's books, as I've always encouraged read-ing in bed. If children think something is naughty or forbidden they much are more likely to do it.

Pippa has commented how much tidier I keep Folie as opposed to our house in England. Of course there is far less junk. Few papers get brought into the house, and even those are stored for lighting fires; no post; no clothes, no clusters of discarded shoes, except those we have brought for our holiday. And the kitchen in particular looks very messy if the washing-up is not done or the table not cleared, as these are the things one first sees on entering, so I expect everyone to help after meals. It is so much nicer to return after an excursion to a neat house. I would love to be tidier at home too, and as most of the heaps are of my own making, it is up to me to keep them under control. It just seems more difficult in England, when there are so many different activities going on and so many demands on our time. Everyone agrees that life does seem slower in France. No one appears to mind waiting while others are served in the butcher's or the *boulangerie*, indeed, it is seen as a good time to catch up on a bit of gossip or to receive the wisdom of the locals on how exactly to cook our piece of meat. They, of course, have no idea of the vagaries of our cooker, so careful timings are somewhat irrelevant. But this relaxed life assumes that one is not trying to earn a living. Friends who have moved permanently to France say that one needs less of everything, fewer clothes, no keeping up with the Joneses. They are, admittedly, not attempting to make lots of money, only to exist in a more laid-back world, but running a B&B or letting part of your property as a *gîte* brings its own stress. We never intended to make 'Folie' a permanent home, merely a very comfortable holiday house, not a simple *gîte*, but to have most of the small luxuries one is used to in England.

Monsieur Coruble, who used to live at 'Folie', must have been a keen gardener. Few rural houses boast the variety of plants that he had grown, including a buddleia, which attracts a multitude of butterflies. The magnolia, which seems to have some flowers on it from spring to autumn, has grown enormously, as I realise when I look at early photos. By the patio, hydrangeas grow so vigorously every year, that they almost prevent access to the terrace I made for summer dining. Hibiscuses grow like a weed, self-seeding wherever they like. Where our neighbours put in the wire fence dividing their chicken run, we have grown a hedge of hibiscus using these seedlings. They seem to survive the most casual method of planting, a spade thrust into the soil, the earth pushed to one side and the plant dropped into the crack. I have planted a vigorous wisteria, which now threatens to engulf the whole of the back of the house each year. It grows at least two metres between each of my visits, and is determined to climb to the roof every three months. Perilously perched on a bending metal ladder, head among the greenery, I chop it all back like mad while trying to avoid the shower of mortar as I pull long strands away from the walls. In a good year, when I have got the pruning right, the long sweet-scented pale purple racemes of flowers make up for all this effort.

A mimosa grew so fast that I had to saw its head off after only a couple of years. It had produced sprays of delicately-scented tiny yellow pompoms all over, one Easter. But it has grown so big that it will have to go as it is now dominating the garden. One rather special tree which I have planted, and which is common in the Corrèze, is the Albizia, or Persian silk tree. They like hot summers and cold, frosty winters, conditions they would have thrived in where they originated and which they get in this part of France. Specimens grow to about twenty feet high in a graceful umbrella shape. The leaves are similar to the acacia, but its flowers are like cup-sized pink powder puffs. I am delighted with the progress of a walnut tree I planted in the lower garden, which now produces a crop of about 6lbs each year. Picking up the fallen nuts can be a dirty business if any of the outer casings are still clinging onto them. It is a powerful dark brown dye. In every orchard in the autumn, one sees bent figures carefully collecting the fallen walnuts into shallow wooden trugs. It is quite easy to miss the nuts among the grass. In fact it is noticeable that the ground underneath walnut trees is the most neatly tended, with few weeds and often harrowed to a fine tilth. Walnuts are too valuable a crop to lose.

By the terrace is a large arum lily, which I love, though some people regard them as funereal. It made a bold subject for an oil painting one summer. The trumpet-shaped flowers are a translucent, greenish-white when the sun shines through them and this is how I painted them, looking up through the plant to the sky. I had the lilies framed to match an oil painting of scarlet oriental poppies, which I grow in England, and the two paintings decorate Vicky's living room. I have been firmly instructed by her that I must never sell them.

Serious physical work was needed to make the shady terrace. This area had had a small pond, which, by the time I acquired the house was dry and overgrown, and the rest was covered with weeds. I filled the pond with stones, bricks, an old sink and whatever solid rubbish I could find, then shovelled earth over it all and laid stone slabs which I found around the garden. Some of these pieces had been steps to the little terrace at the top of the garden. I unearthed more stone from the lawn, where there must have been a path under the washing line which Mme Coruble used. There was just enough stone to cover the area I had cleared, though it had to be carefully laid to make the surface as even as possible; difficult, as many of the chunks were lumpy and bumpy, not at all like proper paving. The next year Tony constructed a wooden pergola with pillars and crossbeams onto which I laid cane matting for protection against the strong summer sunshine. I have tried growing vines over this, but they are not growing fast enough to cover it so far. A wisteria would cover it faster, but probably submerge it altogether if it wasn't pruned violently enough.

Sitting on the terrace one day, taking a well-earned and unaccustomed rest, my gaze was drawn to a stone, out of line with the bottom corner of the front wall of the house. I stared at it, not quite believing my eyes. I bent over, to see whether, upside down, it was what I thought. With hammer and chisel I carefully levered the stone away from the wall, to which it had merely been stuck with cement. Turning it the right way up I was sure that it was a Maltese or Templar cross carved from granite. Its upper arms were short, the lower one long, therefore it had been placed the wrong way up against the wall. Since I knew that inverted crosses are used in witchcraft, I reversed it immediately, propping it up against the pergola, where it remains. Since then I have also found a slightly damaged, but finely carved Corinthian capital, probably from an old church, in a *brocante* up in the hills, which is a lovely companion for the cross.

Along the wall, which holds back the upper garden, I have planted rockroses, lavender, sage and erigeron, a daisy-like rockery plant, which roots into every crevice in the wall and the path if I let it. Pots full of geraniums sit on the steps up to the old front door, and also tumble over a wrought iron pot stand, recast from a Victorian one, which stands near the side gate. An extremely pretty iron and wood bench, bought in a closing-down sale in Chelsea, is placed in front of the new oil store, where it invites weary gardeners to sit a while and stare. Nearby is a fine and valuable stone trough I found in the garden. Planting up the pots is an enjoyable spring task, as it immediately makes the entrance cheerful and the house look lived in. We continued the green theme by painting all the iron-work and the exterior woodwork with a subtle dark matt green paint. The front gate alone took Pippa a whole day as the metal mesh has many facets. Even a white plastic garden table got the green treatment. For all our hard work, both sourcing and constructing, the delays, the hassles and the disappointments, the house is now such a pleasant and relaxing home that we all agree it was worth it.

Geese : Jawlat

Chapter 7
LOCATION, LOCATION, LOCATION…

Location, location, location! is the eternal cry of estate agents everywhere. However, we didn't realise just what a gem we had chosen in the first instance. The price was right. The potential for a cosy home was there. A few minutes' walk brought you to the *boulangerie*. And it was not on a main road. Above all it was peaceful, quiet enough for local workmen to comment. Even in high summer, when there are more visitors to the area and one would expect more cars, Tony and his friend Jack, who comes to stay most years, walk through the village after dinner and lie down in the middle of the bridge to look for shooting stars and satellites.

Later we came to appreciate the fact that our house is not overlooked. We have grown a good screen of trees and shrubs along our boundary, so the only bedroom which might have looked out onto our garden is now well obscured. Part of the house next door had been used as a *gîte* until Mme Chazoule died, but the glum son closed up that half. His mother left the barn opposite our house to the dour son and the main house to his two brothers. After an abortive attempt to sell off the old part, nearest to us, which has nowhere private to put out a chair and is accessed through the front yard of the adjoining newer part, the brothers put the whole house on the market. It has been sold to a near-toothless local resident, who intends to convert it into *gîtes*. There is a huge amount of work to do to make it appeal to the increasing demands of English renters. As there is now so much choice in beautiful glossy brochures, only the very best houses can hope to attract tenants, though maybe he intends to advertise the *gîtes* in France to the less picky French. Hopefully he'll take a long time over the conversion, or give up entirely, realising the depressing enormity of his self-appointed task. The son who had been left the barn was thrown out of his home by his brothers and, not being able to afford to convert the barn that he now owned into flats, also decided to sell, moving to nearby Beaulieu. We were down at La Folie Verte when all these shenanigans were going on, so were able to jump in quickly with a bid for the barn. He rejected our first offer, insisting on the asking price. In order to stop anyone else converting it, putting in windows that would have overlooked our garden and parking cars right in front of our house, we decided we had to buy it, though we have no immediate plans to do any building work ourselves.

Our upper boundary is marked with trees overgrowing an almost completely hidden wall, but at one point it is possible to scramble up a bank onto a steeply sloping field. Sheep used to graze on it under apple, pear and walnut trees, and the remaining meadow grass is still sprinkled with the occasional wild orchid, oregano and other stumpy flowers. The absentee owner has virtually abandoned this field, sometimes allowing a rather aggressive black horse the run of what meadow is left. The rest is covered with rampaging brambles. Its very neglect has increased our privacy, however. Our neighbours, whose well-watered vegetable garden adjoins the wall of the parrot room and runs along our lower garden, are a charming old couple who generously offer me eggs from their hens when I arrive for each visit. We always go through a sort of ritual.

"Hello, how are you?" I say,

"As well as can be expected at our age. Are you here alone?"

"Yes. I have a lot of work to do in the house and garden."

"Oh that's a shame. Are you here for long?"

"Only about 10 days."

"That's a short time. Would you like some eggs?"

"Yes please. That's really kind of you."

We then chat for a few minutes about the weather or their animals and I go on my way, clutching a plastic bag twisted round six newly-laid eggs, still decorated with the odd scrap of straw. As well as the chickens, they keep a pig, geese (for the *foie gras* as well as for eating), turkeys, ducks and rabbits. I am reminded every time I see these rabbits of the poignant film *Jean de Florette*, which I have watched many times. The rabbits, which Jean (Gerard Depardieu's character) tried to keep at his *mas* in Provence, are exactly the same type as my neighbours' russet-coloured ones, large and good-natured. I have never yet summoned up the courage to buy one for the pot. One winter, seeing these elderly smallholders tending their animals in the freezing cold, I asked them why they didn't use fingerless gloves, but they had never heard of such a thing. They received two pairs the week after my return. Whether they ever wear them is another question!

Many of the villagers keep hunting dogs, as there are rabbits, deer and boar living in the woods surrounding our part of the valley. The dogs sometimes are a nuisance with their competitive barks and yelps, but it's all part of country living, just like the occasional obnoxious manure smells or slow tractors cluttering up the back lanes. Licences for hunting guns seem readily available from the Mairie. Pierre, who cuts my grass (when he finds the time), can often be seen kitted up for the hunt at weekends in Autumn. In truth, I think that the jaunts are just a good excuse to get together with his mates. He rarely seems to bring home a kill.

When walking through any village, even the children say a polite and fearless *'bonjour'*, whether they know you or not, a refreshing change from the English habit of averted eyes or the downright rude and pushy behaviour of many youngsters in the street. The adult residents proffer a greeting, but few stand and chat. Rural French villagers keep themselves to themselves, and as an incomer and particularly as a foreigner, it is important to understand their conventions of politeness. You use the formal *vous*, even with your cleaner and her teenagers, who may greet you with four kisses. Grateful thanks must be effusively given for any favour. On one occasion, Monsieur Clouseau, the rabbit keeper, cut my grass. I took a bottle of Pineau de Charentes to him as a way of saying "thank you". He returned the favour by asking me and the girlfriend who was staying with me, to his home for *"une verre"*. This entailed partaking of two glasses of wine, served with *langue de chat* biscuits at 5.30pm. After about an hour we were expected to make our exit. I am again in their debt, and that's the way they like it. Twice I have asked Mme Gravier, in the *boulangerie*, who seems to be one of the most sociable of the villagers, to come up for a coffee. I'm sure she is dying to see the house, but convention seems to preclude her acceptance. I sometimes wonder what the villagers who have seen my house think of what I have done to it. Their own rooms are dark, with brown paint, wallpaper in dark prints, heavy brown furniture, flimsily-made kitchen tables and chairs of metal and plastic. Much of the furniture available in the shops is very dated to our eyes, stuck in the 1950s or 60s. My house is bright, light, fresh and colourful. Maybe they think it garish and impractical. *Chacun à son goût*. (Each to his own!)

In 'Folie' I have some old postcards of the village around the turn of the twentieth century. There were originally three bars (for a population of about 200 at the most), only one of which survives. The cheerful lady, whose teeth are mostly of metal, who runs the last remaining bar, also sells peaches, tomatoes and beans which her husband grows. A whole tray of peaches costs about £4. Some years ago I bought a strong metal sandwich maker at a street market. We make a delicious and fattening pudding with this. *Pain de mie* (a packeted sweet white bread) is buttered and placed butter side down in the metal hollows, then a spoonful of strawberry or raspberry jam is heaped onto one piece of bread and slices of peach are put on top of the jam. The two halves of the sandwich-maker are clipped together, and the sandwich cooked over the gas for a few minutes each side. Served with a sprinkle of castor sugar and a dollop of *crème fraîche*, the result is heavenly.

Another favourite hot pudding to make with peaches is one I discovered in a food article some years ago. Halve and stone the peaches, squeeze some lemon juice over the cut sides to prevent browning, and place in a baking dish. Crush some amaretti biscuits or macaroons (about two per peach), by putting the biscuits in a strong plastic bag and hitting them with a rolling pin, and then tip them into a bowl. Add enough amaretto liqueur, local fortified fruit or nut hooch to moisten the biscuits and stir well. Fill the middles of the peaches with this mixture, making a small mound above each stone-hole. Any left-over filling can be put around the peaches. Pour a little more liqueur into the dish and bake for about 20 minutes. Serve warm with *crème fraîche*. French dinner guests have been extremely complimentary about this pud – one, who'd particularly enjoyed it, admitted afterwards that he'd not been looking forward to eating an English meal. I was glad to be able to repudiate the continental view of us as lousy cooks. The French in fact, rarely bother to make their own puddings, preferring to buy one of the splendid fruit *tartes*, or extravagant mousse cakes produced by every *patisserie*.

Anyway, I digress... as I was saying, 'Folie' is in a fantastic location, with a quiet setting and lovely views from the house over the village rooftops and beyond, to the wooded hills on the other side of the valley. There is also the river, which is ideal for canoeing. All summer there is a regular parade of hired canoes lazily paddling or drifting downstream. At times the current is so fast that very little effort is necessary, while other stretches are so deep and wide that the river runs very slowly. There are five or six sections of rapids between Argentat and Beaulieu, several of which are quite tricky, especially for inexperienced canoeists (most of us!). A stony beach on a curve beside the rapids just below our village has become a favourite spot to watch the antics of these untutored canoeists tumbling out and trying to right their water-filled craft. In fact, it is so shallow at times that the canoes actually scrape on the river-bed. The water is never too fast to be very dangerous, or rather, one is not permitted to take canoes on the river when it is too swift for safety. Anyone falling in over the rapids can easily stand up on the stones, though I did fall in once, having made an awkward jerky movement, further down the river, in still deep water. If Pippa had not learnt, on an adventure holiday in Wales, how to do a canoe rescue, rolling the abandoned boat onto the front of her own, I would have lost it completely. It was so full of water that it nearly sank. As it was, with a life jacket on, I was able to bob to the shore, empty the hull, ignominiously climb back in, to much ribald laughter from the girls, and paddle on downstream.

A tree-shaded campsite a mile or so down river provides a relatively safe place to swim or launch the canoes. I have gathered lots of old pairs of tennis shoes in child to giant sizes from jumble sales, which I leave in a box for general use. Shoes are advisable for either canoeing or swimming as the river-bed is muddy at the edge, and further in the stones are slippery. I need a continuous supply of these old shoes, as they usually fall apart after a couple of years, their soles either turning to rubbery dust or flapping off as you clamber out of the water. Near the bank, the river is slow enough to paddle the canoes upstream for several hundred yards, though in the middle it flows faster and it takes some effort to swim across. Towards the far bank are some large smooth rocks sticking out of the water, and it is a popular occupation to swim across to these. I am not a very strong swimmer so if I aim some 20 yards upstream of the stones, I will be gradually swept down onto them. So far it's always worked. Only when it is extremely hot do I want to go in at all, as the water is always freezing. A long way upstream the river rises in the snowy mountains of the Auvergne, and even in Summer it is still melt-water that has passed through the deep reservoirs and dams of the now flooded gorges of the Dordogne. Generally the fast-flowing water has not absorbed much sunshine and remains very cold. It doesn't seem to put off the kids, who splash about at the campsite and further down at Beaulieu with impunity. The Dordogne valley is noted for its beauty, but the stretch either side of us has to be some of the prettiest, with scenery varying from rocky cliffs, to open meadows and groves of walnut trees. West of Beaulieu the hills rarely get so close together. Often there is a steep scarp on one side and a wide plain on the other. As the river nears Bordeaux the landscape gets flatter, and to my eye, less striking. We think our end's better!

Beaulieu is one of the best reasons for having a house in the Corrèze, as it is an ancient town with a renowned Romanesque abbey church. The word 'Roman' is often used confusingly in France to describe a Romanesque, religious building of the 10th-12th centuries. Tourists must frequently wander vainly around villages searching for the Roman remains they think they have seen advertised on road signs. You approach the imposing Abbatiale from one of the four large squares in Beaulieu. Its huge carved tympanum illustrates the many-headed beasts and sea creatures described in the Apocalypse, the figure of Christ in Majesty flanked by angels blowing trumpets and the Apostles. The dead, who have been redeemed, are pushing up the lids of their coffins on Judgement Day. Either side of the porch are worn sculptures of prophets and Daniel in the lion's den. The style of this impressive tympanum is simi-

The imposing Abbatiale in Beaulieu

lar to carvings at the Abbeys at Souillac, Carennac and Moissac, among others, and the same group of stonemasons from Toulouse probably worked on all of them. A square tower at one end of the church is topped by a smaller, later clocktower set askew to the main one. Centrally, over the transept, is a larger square tower surmounted by an octagonal one. Inside the atmosphere is sombre – although the space enclosed is vast, the amount of light which penetrates is negligible. Massive columns support the roof and the side chapels are dark. The interior is strangely lacking in decoration. Few capitals are carved, though there are several unsophisticated and charming representations of lions. Obviously the sculptors who did the magnificent carvings on the tympanum were not responsible for the inside. One capital, which amuses me, is a weedy man with very large feet and a tiny head fending off two large but apparently unaggressive animals.

The name 'Beaulieu' comes from the Latin *'bellus locus'* meaning 'beautiful place'. With its lovely riverside position and the fine buildings that line the bank, including the much photographed 'Chapelle des Penitents', Beaulieu is well named. The chapel has an open bell-tower, characteristic of many churches in this area, though there are no bells hanging in the openings any more. It is now used for art exhibitions and occasional concerts. Recently it survived a disastrous fire, which destroyed a pretty old cottage next door. Nearby, with a view to the river, is a fine galleried house currently used as the Youth Hostel. Among the other townhouses is a tall and elegant mansion (currently vacant), decorated on the outside with wonderful Renaissance carvings. It had been bought by an English man and in the process of restoring it he fell down the stairs and died. His mother inherited it, and has sadly neither continued the restoration, nor put it back onto the market.

Very little is left of the old town walls, but the outline of them is echoed with a curved road, lined on one side with grand three or four-storey houses, their front doors approached by exterior staircases with elaborate wrought-iron

balustrades and balconies. Their gardens are sufficiently shel-
tered to nurture exotic palm trees, oleanders and banana
plants. In the centre of the town, surrounding the Abbatiale,
clean, tidy, stone-paved streets are flanked by many beautifully restored stone, or timber-framed houses in the less frequently trod back alleys. Some are less neatly plastered, neglected
and unrepaired. I find it strange that the local council has not
compelled the owners of several decaying houses in the square
right opposite the Abbatiale to restore them. On all the other
sides of the square, the buildings have been carefully repointed and re-roofed, but these derelict houses have broken windows, loose shutters and peeling plaster, exposing the inner
laths. Rotten timbers and eroded stone pillars barely support
the overhanging upper floors. All very sad-looking.

A regular Friday market or *foire* attracts shoppers from miles
around. The *foires* have more stalls than the *marchés*. There are
clothes, old and new, chair caners, traders from North Africa
with their beads and leather goods, as well as the usual fruit
and veg – beautifully arranged and fresh – olives, bread, fish,
meat, wine, honey, flowers and plants. Three of the town
squares are colourful with bright striped canopies over the
heaped-up goods for sale. Shoppers from the town and outlying villages flood in to make their modest purchases. Cheeses,
sold from well-stocked travelling vans, attract long queues.
Smallholders may arrive with half a dozen chickens or ducks,
a few bunches of carrots, a basket of walnuts, or some farm-
fresh goat's cheese. Eggs, still stuck with bits of straw, will be
carefully placed in a plastic bag, the top just twisted round —-
no cardboard egg-boxes – a delicate responsibility for the designated carrier. Everyday shopping is a pleasure. Even Tony,
who in England is a vociferously reluctant shopper, enjoys the
old-fashioned style of Beaulieu's shops. Anyone entering a
boulangerie or butcher's greets all the other customers with a
murmured *"Bonjour, messieurs, mesdames,"* and even I, as an
irregular regular, am recognised in several shops and my
length of stay and welfare are enquired upon.

The ability to travel further afield for excursions is one of the best things about the area. North, south, west or east – there is so much to see and do. We can drive west along the Dordogne, visiting the prehistoric sites of the River Vezère. This part of central France has been described as the cradle of Neanderthal man, though he was probably a refugee from Africa originally. One of the earliest skeletons was discovered closer to my home, at Chapelle des Saintes, near Vayrac, where a museum has recently been established.

In the Vezère valley are exposed rock shelters and cave systems where primitive man lived. Here is the amazing replica of the Lascaux cave, with its incredibly lifelike paintings of animals, bison, a bull, horses and deer, which has been cunningly reconstructed within the very same hill as the original. Conservationists closed the real Lascaux cave some years ago to all but the most erudite researchers, as the breath from visitors was causing moulds to grow, obscuring the paintings on the walls and ceiling. One descends along a passage cut into the wooded hillside, through a small exhibition showing how the new cave was built, and the materials and methods of the painters of more than 15,000 years ago. They worked by the light of simple oil lamps, perched on wooden scaffolding, using ground-up clays, stone and charcoal to obtain a limited range of colours. As soon as you enter the painted passageways you forget it is not the original one. The curves of a horse's flank follow the contours of the rock itself. A bulge in the stone emphasises the strength of a bison's head. Artists of today are envious of the confident line these 'primitive' draughtsmen produced with apparent ease.

Within a day's drive there are many old fortresses and chateaux. Closer at hand is the famous Saturday morning market in Sarlat, which specialises in regional produce. Sarlat itself is a fascinating old town with some most unusual architecture including the amusingly named device called a squinch, where the corner of a building is cut away to allow pedestrians to pass under the overhanging half-arch now supporting the upper floors. Near this neat bit of town planning is an old well, actually a spring-fed cistern approached down several slippery moss-covered steps. The ingress of the water is invisible and the level always stays the same however this is *eau non potable* (non-drinkable). There is probably pollution from the buildings standing right on top of it. Another few steps take one to a raised area surrounded by wisteria-entwined towers and railings where the town's *raison d'être* – three fine geese – are displayed, cast in bronze; always the spot where tourists want to be photographed, either sitting on their backs or pretending to herd them.

There are fine Renaissance buildings decorated with detailed carvings, and the mysterious 12th century 'Lanterne des Morts' behind the church. Several of these tall conical buildings survive in the region. Exactly what their purpose was is unknown. It is mooted that the dead were placed inside the towers for a period of mourning, and a fire was lit on the floor of the top storey as an honour, like the Eternal Flame used at symbolic burial places for war-dead today. But at Sarlat the upper room had no access, so it would have been difficult to light a fire in there as a visible sign to distant observers. Behind the church is a small churchyard with tombs decorated with swords, probably predating the existing 15th century church. They look like the gravestones of Templars, and as there are many other Templar connections in South-West France, it isn't unlikely.

According to the season, the market offers walnuts, truffles, *ceps*, strawberries, and of course *foie gras, pâtés*, and *confit* (duck or goose legs and breasts preserved in their own fat). This, whether from a can or a jar, is one of the things I regularly bring home. It makes an almost instant dinner party dish. Open the container. Place it in a saucepan of barely simmering water, which should come about half way up the sides of the jar or can. Pour the melted fat into a bowl. Either bake or grill the joints until hot and slightly crisp. Sauté some potatoes with a little chopped garlic, using several tablespoonfuls of the reserved fat. Keep the rest of the fat in a covered jar in the fridge for roasting potatoes another time. Sprinkle the sautéed potatoes with chopped parsley before serving. Traditionally no vegetables are served with *confit*, though some green beans or a simple green salad with a tangy dressing will cut the rich flavours of meat and potatoes. A few glasses of red Cahors wine goes down well with this dish and acts medicinally, so the docs now tell us (as if we need any persuasion to enjoy a glass or two). It is a strange thing that the people who regularly eat the fatty, rich food of Perigord, with quantities of cakes and flans, and generous amounts of red wine, seem to suffer less from the heart diseases which plague the English. *Vive la France* and its delicious food.

Further west along the riverside are many imposing castles including Beynac and Domme as well as dangerously-sited villages such as La Roque Gageac, crouching under sheer or overhanging rock faces.

Even though we did not choose to live in Brit-land we still like to visit these splendid places. What treasures we have all around us.

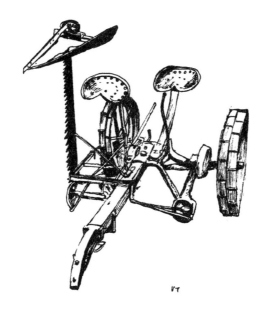

Chapter 8

NORTH, SOUTH AND EAST

East of our district lies the Auvergne, with a totally different landscape to explore. The huge area of the Massif Centrale was turbulently volcanic in the distant past, and mountains rise high enough for skiing. Aurillac, known as the coldest town in France, is the gateway to this region. One exciting way for us to get there is by train from Biars, a small, ugly town about eight miles away. The council there has created a strange modern sculpture from redundant railway tracks, painted in bright colours and exploding out of a former water cistern like a firework. The train mostly runs beside a river, the line tunnelling through dramatic and beautiful outcrops of rock. The whole route is invisible other than on this train, as there is no road closely following the river. In the summer the fields of the Auvergne beyond Aurillac are full of wild flowers, including tall yellow gentians which, only because of the trumpet-like shape of the florets, resemble the low-growing intensely blue gentians of the Alps. There are licensed collectors of these plants, the arm-thick roots of which are used to make a revolting liqueur called Suze or Gentiane, which tastes like the worst medicine you can imagine. Many other rare plants grow on the steep bare slopes of extinct volcanoes, popular with walkers. Towns, like Salers, in the Auvergne have a distinctive serious character of their own as they are often built of the local dark volcanic rock. To the north-east lies Bort les Orgues, named after the clusters of vertical basalt stones which look like organ pipes, similar in structure to those in the Hebrides and Sicily.

North of us, in the Creuse, are some other completely different natural rock formations called the Pierres de Jaumâtre. Trees have grown in such close proximity with the vast rounded, lichen-spattered stones that they sometimes appear to split the rocks apart. Their trunks curve and bend like lianas in a jungle. Many of the sombre towns of this region are at a high altitude and the houses seem to huddle together for protection against the weather, which can be quite different to places a mere 50 miles south. Snow flurries often sweep over between patches of clear sunshine until well after Easter. It seems a truly forgotten and backward part of the country; a complete contrast to the bustle and colour of the more well-known tourist destinations only an hour away.

Throughout France vestiges remain of the ancient pilgrimage routes to Compostella in Northern Spain, where relics of James, one of the fishermen who were disciples of Jesus, are revered in the crypt of the great elaborate 12th century church. After Christ's Ascension all the apostles dispersed and James is believed to have reached this part of Spain while continuing his preaching. When James unadvisedly returned to the Holy Land, where Christians were by then being persecuted, he was captured and beheaded by Herod. It was common practice for martyrs' bodies to be rescued during the night by secret believers and given a Christian burial. James' remains appear to have been moved several times, but are said to have been brought back by boat to northern Spain several centuries later. His body was loaded onto a wooden cart drawn by two oxen, who stopped walking after half a day, so the body was interred there in an old Roman stone tomb they conveniently found at the same spot. People have been making pilgrimages to this place since the year 814 when a bright star, shining over a field, is believed to have led to the discovery of a tomb containing the remains of three bodies, thought to be James and two companions. A church was built over the burial site and later was enlarged several times until the present vast, highly-decorated cathedral was erected. Pope Leo XIII authenticated the bones in 1884 and so revived the mediaeval pilgrimage.

Many Christians still make this journey, carrying with them James' symbol of a scallop shell. In order to qualify as a true pilgrim to Compostella, travellers must either walk a certain distance or, today, are allowed to cycle. They are issued with a certificate that is officially stamped at each of the designated stops before reaching their goal. The best hotel in town offers three meals to each of the first ten pilgrims to knock at its door every day, but they are fed in the kitchen! Churches, such as that at Loubressac, along the many routes that converge in South-West France before crossing the Pyrenees at the Pass of Roncesvalles, frequently have St James' scallop motif carved around the doorway. In the little towns along the way, inns dedicated to St Jaques de Compostella still serve a few dedicated pilgrims, though they actually are more likely nowadays to be serving atheistic tourists. One such inn can be found just north of the Dordogne at the famous tourist village of Collonges la Rouge – *'Rouge'* because of the glowing red sandstone from which it is all built.

Collonges is one of the rare towns in the region that is not despoiled by festoons of telephone wires and electricity cables hung on ugly concrete posts. Some years ago the town council and the residents decided to bring new life to their declining

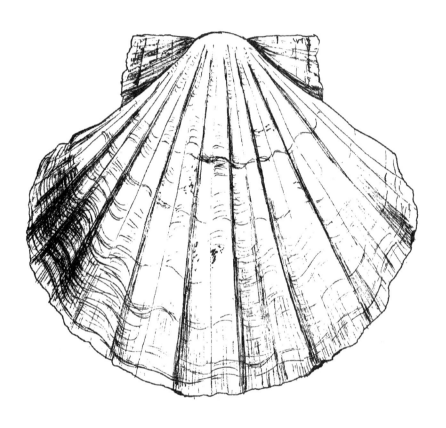

James' symbol of a scallop shell

and decaying village. They deliberately chose to make the whole place a tourist attraction, and boy... have they succeeded! Early morning or evening, when the sun makes the stones truly glow, or out of season, are the only possible times to visit this lovely village. In order to restore the historic feel to Collonges, all the wires were relaid underground and the posts removed. If only the French would do this everywhere! The main road past the village entrance sports a number of sleeping policemen, to prevent through traffic causing accidents to the multitudes who come to wander in the pretty streets and buy up the craft shops. Several car parks have been established for both cars and coaches. All the red sandstone buildings with their steep *lauze* roofs have been beautifully restored. There are several good restaurants and a chapel with a permanent display about the conservation work the residents undertook. The church is remarkable for its twin naves. Possibly the second nave was added just to enlarge the capacity for the congregation. However, I was informed that Catholics and Protestants shared the church. Presumably they agreed on different service times. One side, for the Catholics, is characteristically ornate, with a dominating altarpiece in carved and gilded wood. There is not much ornamentation on the simpler Protestant side. The most famous house in the village is known as 'The House of the Mermaid'; to one side of the entrance, at eye level, is a carving of a seductive mermaid, brush and mirror in hand. It is possible there was a merman on the other side, but as the sandstone is very soft, whatever was there has worn away. What amuses me is that 'mermaid' used to be a common term for a whore. No wonder she looks so enticing.

South of us, one finds the department of the Lot. Here, another great pilgrimage site on the Route de Compostella is only about 50 minutes' drive away. Rocamadour was probably named after an enigmatic character, St Amadour, whose identity has never been established. What is very strange is that when builders were digging a grave in 1166 near the threshold of the Chapel of the Virgin they found human remains already buried in a niche in the rock. These were thought to be those of Zaccheus, a disciple of Jesus, who fled to France after the crucifixion with his wife, Veronica. She was the woman who, during the procession to Calvary, wiped Jesus' face with a towel upon which His image was imprinted. After Veronica's death, Zaccheus became a hermit and may have lived and died in this wild and dry valley of the Alzou, the river having disappeared underground. In the Langue d'Oc, the old language of the region, the phrase *'roc amator'* means 'he who likes the rock', so this interpretation may have been the origin of the place name. Whatever its beginnings, Rocamadour is one of the most remarkable sights in the whole of France. Viewed from a terrace at L'Hospitalet, high above and to one end of the valley, you can't help but be awestruck by its churches and monasteries tucked perilously into a vertical cliff, above which are 14th century ramparts protecting the chaplains' residence which was added to the huddled buildings in the 19th century. Numerous rock falls over the centuries have demolished some of the buildings, most of which have recently been carefully and sensitively restored. From the shops full of commercial tat, which line a single narrow street packed with tourists in the summer, steps lead up to the chapels. Fossil shells, harder than the surrounding stone, stand proud of the vertiginous worn steps. Formerly, true pilgrims would have climbed up on their knees. Even on foot it is quite a haul.

Embedded in the rock face above the doorway of the Chapelle Notre-Dame is a great iron sword; the legendary Durandel, belonging to Count Roland, hero of a series of skirmishes in 778 against the Saracens. He claimed that its jewelled handle contained relics, a tooth belonging to St Peter and part of the Virgin's dress, among other items. Looking at the rusty, simple hilt today, this part of the story seems unlikely. There was a real Count Roland, but the truth of his life became muddled up with the battles of Charlemagne. The story tells that when surrounded by his enemies, at the Pass of Roncevaux in the Pyrenees, Roland tried to break his sword to prevent it being used by the infidels against his own men. Failing to destroy it, he prayed to the Archangel Michael (the angel who always triumphs over evil), and threw the sword to him, whereupon it pierced this cliff at Rocamadour, some 200 miles from where it was thrown. A likely story indeed!

The chapel of Our Lady is hung with small votive offerings and, more obscurely, with several model boats, gifts from grateful penitents. From the ceiling hangs a primitive iron bell dating from the 9th century, which foretells of miracles, and also rings of its own accord when shipwrecked sailors call on Our Lady of Rocamadour to save them. This bell and the model ships link this site with the Breton village of Camaret-sur-mer, which also has a chapel dedicated to Our Lady of Rocamadour. Many visitors come to see, or pay homage to the black virgin, a small Mother and Child carving, formerly sil-ver-plated, though this is now quite hidden by the deposits of candle smoke. She is hard to see in the gloom, but she is clothed, as are so many religious sculptures in French church-es. Even with all the visitors, many of whom ignore the notices in all languages to keep silent, the place has a moving atmos-phere. The composer Poulenc was so affected by a spiritual revelation in 1936 at Rocamadour, that he devoted much of his life to composing religious music, including a choral work dedicated to 'La Vierge Noir'. He is remembered with a small museum in the chapel complex. At La Folie Verte I have a col-lection of books about France, mostly about the Lot, the Dordogne and the Auvergne. One of them, dated around the turn of the 20th century, refers to Rocamadour as "a dirty place, formerly a pilgrimage site, but now a poor place, with nowhere to eat and nowhere to stay". What a difference to today's heaving crowds, packed restaurants and busy shops in the summer. Though I have to admit that there are probably few real pilgrims today it is definitely a place to visit out of sea-son, when it regains a little of its former mystical atmosphere.

A similar village, though with fewer legends connected with its history, dramatically dominates a bend in the river Lot.

Perched on the top of a formidable 262 ft high cliff is the golden-walled, red-roofed St Cirq la Popie. The church here is plain, solid and rather neglected inside. Streets in the compact village are full of twists and turns, with nice little craft shops continuing the tradition of the artistic residents, who once included the writer André Breton. There is an interesting small museum in the remains of the chateau, full of the paintings and collections of Rignault, who donated his possessions to the *département*. A good restaurant, on the approach road, commands the best view of the whole site – if you can manage to bag one of the roadside tables.

Elsewhere in the Lot are vast caves full of stalactites and stalagmites. At Padirac there is the biggest sinkhole in Europe, 325 feet across and 247 feet down. This great chasm, legend says, was created by the devil, who mocked St Martin for failing to save any souls, whereas he, Satan had collected a sackful. The devil challenged St Martin's mule to cross an obstacle he would create, and then, stamping his foot, he caused the massive hole to open up. The mule jumped right over it and the devil returned to hell down the hole he had made, leaving the sack of souls with St Martin.

One descends by lift or steps, 455 of them, past the fern encrusted walls into the depths of the earth, where the real, if unromantic reason for the hole's existence is made clear. In the middle of the floor is a towering heap of fallen rubble, debris from the roof-fall of a gigantic cavern long ago. After a short walk, tourists are punted in a narrow boat on the clear waters of a great underground lake, past a giant, pendulous stalactite whose point nearly dips into the water, to where the spectacular caverns begin. The 'Salle du Grand Dome' is an impressive 295 feet from floor to roof. The dome cannot be many metres of rock below the Causse de Gramat. I'm always a little nervous in these underground caves as evidence of rockfalls and tumbled stalactites which have sheered and crashed off the lofty ceilings are all around. At least we are seeing these amazing sights with discreet fixed lighting. For those of us with any sort of fear of the dark or claustrophobia, the idea of investigating the often water-filled tunnels and passages that speleologists delight in, fills us with horror. It's amazing when you realise that Padirac was discovered in 1889 and consider the sort of lights Edouard Martel and his fellow cavers would have been carrying.

At Lacave the extensive cave system was discovered in 1902 by one of Martel's students. Rare fluorescent concretions are cleverly lit to cast reflections, like a thousand fairy lights, in a shallow lake. In the Salle des Merveilles are hundreds of extraordinary and delicate eccentrics, formations which grow at strange branching angles as the dripping water has been gently blown by light winds penetrating the caves from the outside world.

Pech Merle is blessed with both stalactite formations and paintings, about 30,000 years old. These magnificent caves are open at the moment, to limited numbers of visitors each day, though there is talk of closing them, since they too are suffering from moulds. As in Lascaux the drawings of horses, bison and deer are incredibly fresh, and the line so confident, one would be hard pressed to repeat their technique today. Cleverly, the artists used the undulations of the natural rock to emphasise the swelling of a flank, or the structure of an animal's head. What significance these drawings had for primitive man we can never know, but their lives seemed remarkably close to mine when I saw the stencil of a small, broad hand, stubby fingers outspread, made by blowing powdered pigment around each finger and the palm. The stencil was exactly the same size and shape as my own hand. In the bed of a dried-up river, natural marbles of limestone have formed where stones became imbedded in a hole. The churning water, unable to dislodge them, swirled them round and round for hundreds, if not thousands of years until they formed into a perfect globe. Even more strange is an almost cone-shaped object about five inches in diameter, which was formed, pointed side down, in the same way. It has been lifted out and left beside the hole it came from. It looks just like the classic description of a flying saucer.

Apart from the wonderful foods that grow freely in the fertile soils of Quercy, there are a number of other interesting crops which fill the fields with colour at various times of the year. Sunflowers are very important as a great deal of sunflower oil is produced from them, and the residue from the crushed heads is used to feed cattle. In French their name is very appropriately *tournesol*, or 'turn to the sun,' which is exactly what the flowers do all day, swivelling their cheerful faces east to west. Just below Curemonte is a large open-sided shed, used for drying great clusters of the long pointed leaves of tobacco which is grown throughout the Corrèze and Lot. Whether it is sold commercially for Gitanes or Gauloises I don't know. It is certainly pungent at close quarters. The plants stand at least five feet tall with insignificant clusters of white flowers at the top. From a distance they resemble sweetcorn, but close up one sees the leaves of the corn are much smaller and the plants considerably taller.

Corncobs are harvested for cattle feed and stored in long wooden cages built on stilts to deter rats, with sides made of chicken wire to allow the cobs to dry but not to rot. Not all farmyards are tidy, by any means, with their steaming smelly muck-heaps and abandoned old-fashioned machinery everywhere, but the corn-cages look very neat, as do the immaculately arranged stacks of firewood. By every road extensive heaps of logs are piled in graded sizes, often partly covered with tarpaulin, and left to season for a year or so. It is probably a criminal offence to remove any wood from someone else's heap, and the country code of honour is such that no one does.

The landscape of all the country I can easily travel to in a day is undulating, if not hilly, mostly farmland. I may have a romantic view of the district of Quercy (its old, but often-used name), but I think that its beauty and variety justifies my rose-tinted view. Even ruined buildings look as if they are so deep-rooted that nothing would ever dislodge them from their chosen spot. The majority of buildings are old, weather-worn and full of character. Modern additions are restricted in number and location. Little disturbs the eye. In each of the surrounding departments are intriguing towns, fascinating museums, art galleries, churches with magnificent cloisters, castles, rivers, and, above all, superb scenery. The whole is blessed with a climate that for at least eight months of the year is considerably warmer and somewhat more reliable than our own. Do I need anything else to convince my readers that I chose a good location?

Futuroscope
VT

Chapter 9
IS TRAVELLING EXPECTANTLY
BETTER THAN ARRIVING?

Definitely not, as far as I am concerned. I try to make each journey as short, in time, as possible, though I take sensible rests and stops so as not to fall asleep with the monotony of motorway driving. I have discovered that listening to books on tape makes the miles fly by. It is reassuring to realise, however, that when facing a difficult motoring situation, the automatic reaction is to concentrate on the driving. A few minutes of the story have gone by, unregistered. Music may be pleasant and easy on the ear, but it is soporific and doesn't stimulate the mind. I buy cheap tapes in charity shops and really don't mind what the story is, so I have been intrigued by murder mysteries, fascinated by historical novels, been swept along by books which have been made into films and listened to all sorts of stories for which I would normally neither get the time nor opt to read.

When we started going to our house there were not many motorways that went in our direction. Originally, looking at the map, there seemed little to choose between one route and another. After our first trip by hovercraft we decided that Portsmouth was easier to reach than Dover, so we began taking the night boat to Le Havre. Timing our arrival at Portsmouth has become an art, too early and the car is loaded onto an upper deck, which is hoisted above the next deck. Getting away at the French end can be delayed by up to half an hour if you get put there. The P&O boats are infinitely better than they used to be. It's now like taking a mini cruise. You almost don't feel you are on a boat, unless you go on deck. We like to watch the process of casting off. The captains have amazing skill at turning the boat in its own length, before powering out of harbour past naval vessels in all sizes up to the biggest aircraft carriers and past some historic three-masted sailing ships. The boat leaves behind the pubs, churches and restaurants of the small part of the old town not bombed in the War and then slides out of Southampton Water into the night, by which time I'm usually tucked up ready to sleep. But if you don't want an early night, have the energy, and are not doing *all* the driving next day, there is a cinema, casino, restaurants and live entertainment to enjoy.

Each cabin is equipped with a loo and shower. The bunks are comfortable, if rather narrow, but turning too energetically in the night can result in elbows or knees bruised on the cabin walls. The duvets are adequate but the pillows are lumpy (regular travellers can be spotted as they take their own pillows from their cars to their cabins). Through the influence of friends who I unexpectedly met one evening on the car deck, I now travel club class, and not only enjoy a large cabin with a proper double bed, tea and coffee making facilities, the use of a secluded lounge with free newspapers, hot drinks, juice and shortbread biscuits, but also a very substantial breakfast brought to the cabin. This latter pleasure is tempered by the staff, who insist on waking everyone at least an hour before docking. I try to ignore their persistent knocking and set my alarm clock for a mere 20 minutes before arrival, as it is just long enough for a quick wash, dress, and gobbled breakfast of coffee and croissant. The yoghurt and juice I save for lunch.

The sun is rarely up by the time we leave the boat. Many mornings I have been greeted by mist or rain. Driving in the gloom and wet is not one of my favourite activities. A few miles from the port, just out of town, the road, built on reclaimed land, follows a low range of white cliffs to the left. On the right is one of the biggest petrochemical works in Europe. A sulphurous stink pervades the air. Chimneys belch out smoke, steam and fumes, or shoot flames into the murky sky as if with the fires of hell. Shiny metal pipes, tubes, chimneys and tanks are ablaze with multicoloured lights like a multitude of demonic Christmas trees. Beyond the Pont de Tancarville, alongside the immensely wide ship canal, is another huge industrial area and scattered along this road are small hamlets and dairy farms, the cows grazing unconcerned in the disgustingly polluted fields. You wonder if the milk would be tainted with the sulphur that fills your nostrils for miles.

Leaving these dreadful smells as quickly as possible we used to head towards Le Mans, then through Poitiers, Limoges and Tulle before the final 25 miles of small cross-country roads. Much of Northern France is very flat and dull and this route took up to nine hours' actual driving time. There was no motorway and not much was dual carriageway either. Its only excitement was passing the spectacular modern buildings of Futuroscope at Poitiers, where a huge theme park is devoted to film in every form one can imagine. Once we stayed overnight nearby and spent a fascinating day viewing 3D films, some so realistic you feel you could put your hand out and capture the objects apparently flying out of the screen over your head. Other screens are as big as a football field or are in IMAX format, surrounding the audience with 360° of action. One film terrified us all, as we seemed to be realistically careering out of control down a mine shaft, the trucks leaping over gaps or screeching to a halt and abruptly reversing when something else hurtled towards us. The seats moved accordingly, amplifying our terror. In another cinema, images were projected below your feet as well as on a normal screen in front, making you feel as if you too were a butterfly skimming over the treetops or dipping down to the river. The buildings which house at least 20 different ways of demonstrating the art of film are revolutionary in their design. One is a leaning, blue glass, spiky crystal, another a great globe. You need to spend several days there to experience all the site has to offer, including a light and sound show in the evening. But for us, the house was calling.

Having decided that the western route was not very successful, we then plotted another which appeared equidistant on the map. This proved much better. I now drive towards Paris and drop off the motorway past Evreux. Before a new main road was built I used to divert before Dreux, through some pretty villages, before rejoining the deadly boring, straight, mostly single track N154 to Chartres. With recent road improvements the pretty option has been blocked off, but the main road is much quicker. At Chartres I always stop for coffee and some tasty pastry, then stretch my legs around the super shops, usually finding myself tempted with some clothes from M&S Modes. Their logo is a neat take-off of Marks and Spencer, even using the same green, but their clothes are up-to-date, and in all sizes from 8-24. Even those of generous build, like me, can find moderately-priced modern clothes to fit.

If I am travelling with someone who has never visited Chartres before we pop into the cathedral. It has to be my favourite cathedral of all those I have seen in France. The exterior is an exuberant riot of statuary (more than 2000 figures) and elaborate flying buttresses. An unusual clock is set on the outside of a side chapel on one corner, above which a redundant sundial is cradled in the arms of an angel. Each part of the exterior seems to have been designed by a different architect. The most obvious anomaly is the totally unmatching pair of spires. One is in florid gothic style, the other, added shortly after, is much simpler. Would architects today have the courage to build two entirely different towers, just because the fashion had changed? Originally the building was designed with a shorter nave than is seen today. A fire in 1134 burnt down the towers and western porch. Because the west front with its partially rebuilt towers was not by then connected to the nave, it was the only part to survive a second devastating fire in 1194, which destroyed much of the old city as well. There is little symmetry in the façade, where even the great rose window is not placed centrally over the portico.

Inside you are immediately struck by the glowing colours of the 175 windows filled with superb and brilliantly coloured stained glass, mostly dating from before 1220. The floor rises in a gentle slope to a set of steps where the nave begins. Strange unfinished columns, the spring of the arches curiously truncated, are a visible sign of the builders' change of mind. Chairs now obscure the inset white and blue stones, which mark out a so-called labyrinth on the floor. It is in fact one continuous path with no dead ends – not a true maze. This was a device used in many cathedrals as an aid to contemplation: one follows the narrow path, head bowed, to the centre which represents God. Strangely, in the middle of the design, there used to be a metal plate incised with the legend of Theseus, King of Athens, who was sent to Crete as one of the yearly tribute of men and girls demanded by King Minos. Wall paintings in the Palace of Knossos show these young people skilfully leaping over bulls like trained acrobats. Ariadne, daughter of King Minos, befriended Theseus, giving him a ball of string to help him find his way into and out of the underground labyrinth, where he killed the Minotaur, an aggressive monster, which was half man, half bull. Together they escaped the island but Theseus callously abandoned Ariadne (after all her assistance) on the island of Naxos. Sadly the plaque, with its inappropri-

The Maze in Chartres Cathedral

ate story, was melted down and used as gunmetal during the Napoleonic wars.

There is so much history at Chartres that hundreds of books have been written about its mysteries. From ancient times the hill on which the cathedral stands was a holy place, the site of a spring of pagan religious significance. The Druids certainly worshipped at this grotto, as did the tribe of the Canutes, of whom little is known, but after whom Chartres is named. Buried beneath the nave is a dolmen, which is believed to be on the same alignment as the Church, that is, 47° off the normal east/west axis, the usual orientation for mediæval churches. A carving of a mother and child in age-blackened pear-wood, which some authors think dates from before the birth of Christ, was found on this dolmen. Pilgrims, believing the statue to be of Christian origin, came to worship it at an altar in the crypt.

Later it was moved into the cathedral and the well and stones were deliberately walled up in 1671. During the Revolution in 1793 the statue was destroyed and a replica, which is mediæval in style and probably nothing like the early one, was made in 1857.

One final oddity that fascinates me is a white flagstone, set with a gilded metal plate, in the western aisle of the south transept. It is peculiar, not only because it is an entirely different colour from the surrounding paving, but also because it is positioned at a diagonal to the others. Every year at midday on June 21st, the summer solstice, the stone is illuminated by a ray of sunlight which beams through a circle of plain glass set into the window portraying St Apollinaire. Is it celebrating the pagan midsummer festival? Is St Apollinaire, who was one of the earliest Christian Saints, martyred on July 23rd AD79 in Ravenna, connected in any way with Apollo, the Greek Sun God, who was usually represented with rays of light radiating from his head? In only one of my six books about Chartres, a very erudite tome by Louis Carpentier, can I find any reference to this stone, but he too can give no explanation for its presence.

To return to my mundane southwards journey, the route used to stagger round the painfully slow single carriageway bypass to Chateauroux, with its endless clutter of traffic lights. At each one the road tricks you into thinking things will be better ahead, as it widens into three lanes, which almost instantly and dangerously diminish to just one, until the next set of lights. Thankfully Chateauroux is now bypassed again, by the new A20 motorway which will eventually connect Paris with Toulouse and even, possibly, Barcelona.

Lunch is often a picnic beside the River Creuse at Argenton, in the middle of the town! Pippa found the perfect spot only a few minutes off the main road. A quiet, curved sweep of narrow road beside the river, lined with small limes, has a perfect parapet on which to sit and spread the picnic. All one can hear is the constant swoosh of water over a nearby weir, the twitter

■ The nicely-proportioned main bedroom originally had patterned hessian stapled to the walls on battens (above). The walls are now painted, and the curtains and bedspread, in bright turquoise raw silk, were a gift from a former client (below). Note the artist's model figure on the tiny wall-hung cupboard.

■ *The roof-space (right) had reasonable head-room under the main joists. It was littered with the French owner's abandoned debris including Monsieur Coruble's WW2 military uniform. Rough wooden strips lined the roof for insulation and the area was lit by two tiny skylights.*

■ *The old attic was divided into two bedrooms and the skylights were replaced by Velux windows.*

b

■ The big filthy storeroom (left) which originally housed smelly decaying potatoes, preserving jars, empty paint tins, old chairs and spiders' webs. The window was covered by tattered grey net curtains.

■ The room has now been transformed into the Parrot Room, one of the nicest in the house, peaceful and secluded. I chose bright lime-green striped curtains, jungle print cushions, a plain rug and furnished it with cane chairs and small chests, a navy sofa-bed and an old pine wardrobe and cupboard.

c

■ *The enormous inglenook fireplace in the large living room, pictured when I bought the house (left) and after restoration (below). The flue from the boiler in the room below had been thrust through the floor of the hearth and covered with breezeblocks, and all the stonework had been rendered then painted in red and white to resemble bricks. I had everything stripped out to reveal the original fireplace and the supporting bressummer beam.*

■ The narrow stairs (left), inserted between the main structural beams, had just a few banisters set at right angles to the rail, which made one feel quite sea-sick to look at. An ancient cracked sink, just to the left of the entrance, graced the large kitchen/dining room, which was illuminated by a pair of double French doors at the front, and one small barred window.

■ Full of rustic appeal, the kitchen (right) is now the most-used room in the house. The walls are yellow, the provençal fabric for the curtain mainly red, with some green and yellow, and the chairs are dark green stained wood. I indulge my taste for provençal materials and put a fabric cloth over the red oilcloth-covered table when I am in residence.

e

■ *The previous owner, a widower, had defiled the attractive simplicity of the house (right) with some horrendous 1950s 'improvements'. There was a hideous enclosed porch of glass and metal, like a tall greenhouse, right at the front.*

■ *Below: The builder replaced this with a practical and attractive porch which protects the front door. The walls are in stone, as we had been instructed.*

f

■ *My watercolour of La Folie Verte pictured from the side (left).*

■ *My oil painting entitled "Dolmen II" (below)*

■ *The canvas in the foreground shows my painting of the Chateau of Chinon and the lower town on the curve of the river (above).*

■ *Painting the lilies at la Folie Verte, summer 1991 (above).*

h

of invisible birds, occasional sploshing and squawking of ducks and very few cars. Eight feet below, the river is lively with young trout of varying sizes, scuffling and snuffling after discarded breadcrumbs. Across the river, perched on a rocky outcrop, is a small chapel crowned with an enormous 21 ft high statue of the Virgin, covered in gold leaf. It often occurs to me to wonder what Christ would have made of the ostentatious wealth that the Church displays everywhere, supposedly in His glory. As a simple man from a humble family, who preached poverty, modesty and abstinence, I think Jesus would be appalled at the flamboyance and profligacy shown in most Catholic churches. Not only are the buildings gilded and elaborated, but the vestments and plate cost vast sums, money that perhaps ought to be spent on the needy. Enough of sermons. On with the journey.

Limoges continued to be a real nightmare until a new bypass whizzed through several tunnels to one side of the town, cutting a good 20 minutes off the driving time. My journey continues on the wonderfully empty new motorway to Brive, before diving off, just after a long tunnel, onto side roads for the last 25 miles. The 'home run'! A tremor of excitement accompanies this familiar route passing through little hamlets, up a very steep hill to which my usually overladen car often objects, crawling past the teeming hordes visiting Collonges la Rouge, whose romantic red turrets are glowing, illuminated by the evening sunlight. Past Turenne, heaped on its pyramidal hill, crowned with the round tower of its semi-ruined castle and the perfectly placed umbrella pine tree, through Meyssac, and on, around leaning trees and field-lined roads before the final left turn along the river to my little village. Home!

However, not all of my journeys have been absolutely straightforward. One evening I decided to leave about half an hour earlier than usual as it was a wild and windy night and I wanted to drive a little slower and more cautiously than usual on the familiar A3 to Portsmouth. At the bottom of the hill that winds around the Devil's Punchbowl at Hindhead, at the best of times a slow single carriageway section, I joined a traffic jam of mammoth proportions. Dragging up, inch by inch, the minutes ticking inexorably by, I was confronted 40 minutes later, at the traffic lights, by a policeman indicating that all vehicles should turn left or right. No diversion signs were in place. I had no idea where I was heading and no English map books with me. I later found out that a tree had fallen onto a car on the main road, tragically killing one occupant instantly, the other dying a few days later in hospital, but at the time all I knew was that I was now running late and heading in the wrong direction. Fortunately I was able to call Tony on my mobile and ask for help. He rushed off for a map and phoned back, telling me that I should continue on my back road to Farnham (which I could have reached from home in 20 minutes, if I had known about the blockage), join the A31, then take the M27. Now I was flying along wet, leaf-littered roads, driving much too fast for the road conditions. The wind was tearing leaves from the flailing trees and hurling them at my speeding car. The lorries I passed threw up drenching muddy spray to further obscure my windscreen. I phoned Tony again when I reached the M27 for confirmation of my route.

At 9.50pm, with the boat scheduled to leave at 10.15pm, I arrived at the port, running from my car to interrupt someone else checking in to ask if I was still in time to check in myself. The girl at the desk assured me I was in time, and that, in fact, the boat was delayed by half an hour. She handed me a piece of paper. P&O was informing passengers that due to the storm, it would be a very rough crossing and that if we wished to transfer our booking to the following day – or any other time – we could do so. Having made this immense effort to get to the boat there was no way that I was going to turn around now, or find a hotel for the night. I phoned again to assure Tony of my safe arrival at the port. Much relieved, he told me that someone else had phoned during my cross-country dash and he had yelled, "Where are you now?" at the bewildered friend at the other end of the line. In my cabin on the boat, hearing a door banging which might have been in the corridor outside, I literally staggered up the steep slope to my door, to which I clung as I looked about for the swinging door and tottered back to my bed as the boat heaved and tossed in the storm. My sleeping pill soon kicked in and I heard no more door-banging, nor felt any more movement.

One return journey was marred by a most annoying accident in Le Havre. I was just a few hundred yards from the port, driving carefully on the wet cobbles. The road was wide enough for about six cars, so naturally I considered that I was on a main road. Suddenly, from a side road which joined mine at an angle, a French lady driver shot out at a faster speed than my own. It was one of those "Oh shit!" moments, when you can see exactly what is about to happen but you can do nothing to avoid it. She crunched into my offside wing, the back end of her car then slewing on the wet surface to smash all the way along my driver and passenger's doors. My car was undriveable as she had crushed my wing against the tyre and ruptured my radiator. Someone in a *café* called the police, who shortly arrived to deal with the accident, and a breakdown lorry was called to remove my wrecked car from the middle of the road to the commercial yard of the port. The police stated that she was perfectly in the right to claim *'priorité à droite,'* which is the most ridiculous law existing in France. In most instances it has been rescinded, with many roads now bearing signs to indicate that emerging traffic from side roads does not have priority. But in some towns the law still stands. She was apparently entitled to drive out of her invisible street, without looking onto the main road, at a speed which meant she could not stop. Was I angry? The only trouble she was in was to be driving without having an insurance certificate with her. The police insisted she call her husband to bring their papers to the scene before she was allowed to leave. I had a rather greater problem – how to get home. At the port I was told they had no suitable vehicles to tow my car onto the boat; it had to be driven on. Several English truck drivers were waiting in the office to register their vehicles for the crossing, so I asked them if they had a crowbar in one of their lorries in order to lever the bent wing away from the tyre. I said that I didn't care what damage they did, enough had been done already in the crash; I just wanted to catch the boat. They helped me out and my sad battered car juddered up the ramp and off again the next morning, and eventually I arrived home in the cab of yet another breakdown truck.

Sometimes on my return journeys I used to arrange to have supper with friends who owned a small chateau not far from Rouen, before making the last hour and a quarter run to Le Havre. It was a very pleasant place to take a break, have a cup of tea, walk by the river that ran through their garden and catch up with the gossip. Meanwhile, my hostess also had a million and one things going on at the same time – two daughters at school, the occasional *au pair*, a husband to collect from the station, a language school cum conference centre to organise and cater for, several pets including a pony, a big garden and her husband's parents in a house in the grounds. Supper was, not surprisingly, often a bit delayed, which led to a lot of clock-watching on my part. My departure was frequently hurried, although I never actually missed the boat. One evening Tony was returning with me. Supper was late again, as there had been some business the family needed to discuss. We left at least 10 minutes after our intended time. Two miles up the road there was a roundabout where we should have gone straight ahead to join the Paris/Le Havre motorway, which was only two miles further on. The road was closed off, barred, dug up. Again, no diversion signs were in place. I went round a couple of times frantically looking for some indication of where we should go. Deciding to take the Paris road, in the hope that we would find a road sign, we found this side road quickly leading us onto the motorway. All I could hope for was an interchange before too long, to take us back the way we wanted to go. Ten miles further on I found the interchange. By the time we reached the bit of the motorway near our friend's home we had travelled an extra 20 miles. Our car was a rather under-powered Honda, which didn't appreciate being driven at 105 mph. It started coughing and spluttering, so not daring to risk a complete collapse I dropped to 95mph, which it seemed to reluctantly accept. We reached the Pont de Tancarville, about 20 miles from Le Havre. Time was running out and we had to stop to pay the toll of about 13 francs. Tony had paid with a 50 franc note and was sitting with the change in his lap, fumbling for the purse, when there was a knock at my window. I wound it down and a man outside said,

"Do you think they take credit cards?"

"Not for 13 francs," flashed through my mind, but all I said was, " Here, take this," and grabbing a 20 franc note from Tony's lap thrust it into the bewildered man's hand before driving off at speed. We made it to the port in time to sit in the statutory queue to board. While waiting there was another knock at the window. The same man dropped a selection of coins into my hand saying, "I only needed five francs."

Travelling in France is, more often than not, a pleasure rather than a problem. Some friends who made an overnight journey to Folie stopped for a coffee break at the side of the road during the night. Their son's friend lay down in the middle of the otherwise totally deserted motorway, long enough to be photographed for posterity. Side roads are equally quiet at most times of the day, though not on July 14th, Bastille Day, when everyone's on the move, nor on August 1st when the whole of France piles into their cars and leaves en masse for their holidays. The police are extra-vigilant about speeding and deliberately target English drivers on these days. Most of the time, however, driving in France is like being back in the 1950s, except for the absence of saluting AA motorcyclists. But to answer my own question, there is nothing better than arriving after a long and hopefully uneventful journey, to your own familiar property, to put the kettle on and have a cup of tea while surveying your domain.

Chapter 10

ADVENTURES

Most of the times I visit La Folie Verte, I spend at least one day exploring some new region with my friend Anne, an energetic and enthusiastic lady *'d'une certaine âge'*, as the French would graciously say, who'd initially introduced me to the house. We meet for supper at her home and discuss the following day's route, planning a circuit of about 100 miles. I drive; Anne map-reads. Our trips vary each time. We might decide to look at anything from ancient historical sites to wild flowers. I am particularly interested in prehistoric standing stones, menhirs, circles and dolmen, which abound all over France. I have always believed that dolmen, impressive monuments with three or four upright base stones, onto which massive flat capstones have been hoisted, were chamber tombs, though others say they were constructed for mystical ceremonial purposes. In the British Isles similar structures are frequently buried under mounds, such as those commonly found on Salisbury Plain. There are other exceptional examples of much more complex design, like Newgrange in Ireland.

North of us lies the Corrèze, an underpopulated and remote *département*. Stories of witchcraft and magic still persist, and visiting some of the ancient dolmen, concealed in small clearings in the heavily wooded Monts de Blond, was quite an uncomfortable and spooky experience. These relics of long departed, primitive pagans gave off intense vibes, as if ceremonial rituals have been held around them from their beginnings to the present day. Dolmen vary in size, both in height and in the individual stones used, but their very presence is awe-inspiring to us today. They must have been of profound importance to early man, living as he was in caves or later in wood and mud-built shelters. You can't help but marvel at the effort and community organisation that must have been put into constructing these timeless monuments. Anne and I went to see the amazing, virtually unvisited, Pierre St Martine, on the stony, stubby oak-treed Causse de Gramat. The capstone, which I believe is the largest in France, has a pitted surface but is basically flat and looks like a vast stone table for a family of giants. It is at least 20 feet long and about 1½ feet thick, raised on low supporting stones. It must weigh 20 tons or more. What amazing engineers these apparently primitive people must have been. When we find one of these former chamber tombs, their colourful roughly cut surfaces often remarkably moss-free and fresh, I take photos from all angles to turn into paintings later, in my studio. Although I prefer to paint out of doors, it is not very practical to visit some obscure field every day for a week.

Signposts are usually small and hidden, and even if the dolmen is indicated or marked on the map, we can't always find it. On some occasions we have been shouted at for trespassing, though we had seen no signs and opened no gates. Our explorations have taken us to many ancient, scrubby woodlands. In order to track down some of the more remote stones, I have driven up narrow *'grand randonée'* footpaths, between the rough stone walls, avoiding the biggest of the potholes and the highest of the rocks, and praying for a feasible turning space somewhere, to avoid a perilous journey in reverse. We haven't had a puncture... yet. The Citroën I had one year was perfect for this kind of driving as it had elevating suspension to lift the bottom of the car above the biggest projecting rocks. As the Renault I now drive doesn't have this facility I may have to forgo this easy way of reaching some of our targets. One of our quests took us to a completely abandoned and overgrown village, hidden behind partly-tumbled walls. We skirted the walls, which were highest on the side facing a cleared field. The dolmen, clearly marked on the map, must have been in the middle, but as the brambles arched as high as the rotting roofs, our search came to nothing yet again.

I have read that some dolmen may have had healing properties, particularly if they'd been erected on a Ley line. These invisible lines of force are said to join places of ancient religious importance. In England, Stonehenge, Avebury, and Silbury Hill all lie on well-documented Ley lines, and there are thought to be identifiable straight lines connecting places of occult importance in France as well. Sometimes single standing stones, or menhirs, form part of these lines, or they may be marked by pools of water, or even notches on the skyline of a hill. In mediæval times English churches were often built on significant pagan sites and were often named after St George the dragon-slayer or St Michael, as he was the angel who threw Lucifer out of heaven – good triumphing over evil; Christianity over paganism. This link seems less common in France where few churches bear his name. Paganism flourished in the remote areas of Quercy and witchcraft is still practised in the Monts de Blond and elsewhere, so it's said. There is even a museum of witchcraft at Blancafort. The names of several villages in the Limousin allegedly refer to fairies or the devil.

Having assiduously studied local maps I found few names which have any connection to magic. There is St Feyre, the

Dolmen near Padirac

Chateau of Fayrac and la Fayre, which could all be a references to *fées*, fairies. Then there is a Prieurie de Merlande in a clearing in Feytaud forest; perhaps Merlin's land in a fairy forest? Though the legend of King Arthur and his Knights of the Round Table are thought to be British, the French aristocracy adopted the characters as their own as they personified the ideals of courtly love and chivalry. Chretian de Troyes was the first writer to include the stories about Arthur and Merlin in his romances. But of *sorcières, ombres, esprits* or *fantômes* I found nothing, only hundreds of names ending in 'ac' which indicates a former Roman site. Those Romans got everywhere. Their occupation of this part of France lasted from about 51 to 476 AD. The last Gaullish resistance took place in Uxellodunum, thought to be in Quercy. Although several towns vociferously lay claim to the fame, its exact location is unknown. Ceasar was so angry at the persistent resistance of the Gauls that when they were captured, being the charming fellow he was, he had each prisoner's right hand cut off.

Anne and I drove north one cold April day to find some ancient crosses, some of which she had sought before, after I'd sent her an article referring *to 'Les croix de Lestards'*. Most of the crosses on the list were conventionally decorated with nativity, crucifixion or deposition scenes, with saints or donors supporting the vertical stone. Crosses were usually placed at crossroads to counteract the evil spirits that were thought to lurk there. Criminals were hanged on gallows erected at crossroads, or left to rot in barbaric metal cages, standing or crouching until hunger and thirst killed them, after which the crows would pick the flesh off their bones. No wonder crosses were needed at these sites of true evil. Other crosses seemed less Christian in origin. These strange primitive stone crosses, sometimes carved with eerie moon-like faces and crudely delineated arms and legs, sometimes mark crossroads, but are more often randomly positioned by the side of the road, or are concealed in the woods. One, Anne had said, was hidden among dark, brooding fir trees, well away from the road.

When we made our journey, it was after some severe winter storms which had swept through much of France. This time the figure was nearly visible from the road. The storm had totally flattened a great swathe of trees to the right of the path to the cross. To our left the trees still stood, though their exposed branches had been burnt by the ferocious wind; ahead of us the hunched lichen-spotted figure defiantly remained upright, entirely untouched by the wind or the trees. It seemed as though some uncanny spiritual force had protected it.

Some legends say that the Templars worshipped a disembodied head and used it symbolically in place of a cross. This head, called Baphomet, which has possible links through an esoteric interpretation of some of the Dead Sea Scrolls to the Greek word 'Sophia' (meaning 'wisdom'), is still part of Masonic ceremonies. Celtic stories say that to possess the severed head of an enemy was to possess his strength. Maybe that meant his intellectual strength as well. Some of the crosses we have discovered have heads carved under the crosspieces, or sometimes on the ends. Do these represent Christ's power over his enemies, or a protective representation of shelter for the heads beneath the outstretched arm? Another mystery.

On the same day that we were searching for the Lestards crosses, we stopped near a tall, apparently ordinary, roadside cross, marked on the map but not on the Lestards itinerary. It stood on an unnecessarily large round base, about a metre in diameter, which had deep, clearly carved symbols surrounding the cross. Most of these did not appear to have any well-known religious meaning. In fact they seemed much closer to mystical signs. One was a perfect round sun with radiating points, another a crescent moon enclosing a star. There was a pair of triangles, one pointing up, the other down. These meant nothing to me, until a few weeks later. Whilst reading *Theo's Odyssey*, by Catherine Clement, which the girls had given me for Christmas, I found an illustration of identical triangles, which were described as the Seal of Solomon. The one pointing up represents fire, the other, water. If a line is drawn across the top triangle it now gives the symbol for air, and similarly a line across the base of the downward pointing triangle represents earth. When superimposed, the two triangles contain all the elements and also form the Star of David, so Solomon's power and influence continues with Judaism to the present day. The fourth carving was the only one to show a recognisably Christian sign, as it showed a scallop shell, another link to St James maybe, but an odd companion for the other carvings.

On this same day we also discovered a church with a thatched roof, extremely unusual at the best of times, but more so when everything else around is slate or stone roofed. From here we climbed a steep hill in search of yet another cross. This time we were disappointed to find just a few scattered pieces of stone that may or may not have been what we were looking for. But that is the nature of the hunt. Frequently the maps are wrong, but it doesn't deter us. The pleasure is in the adventure.

Other days we take a new route, or an old one we have not driven at that time of year, in search of wild flowers. Anne is an expert on identifying orchids. Their clustered florets need very careful study to identify a specimen as a military, a man or a monkey orchid. Bee and fly orchids are so realistic that they confuse flying insects who vainly attempt to mate with the flowers, thereby transferring pollen from one to another. Very clever! There are many more types of orchid and with someone as knowledgeable as Anne, who knows the kind of terrain they are likely to inhabit, the hunt is rarely fruitless. One of the most dramatic forms is the lizard orchid, whose trailing green flowers dangle off its 18-inch stem. Sometimes our walks take us to a waterfall or an unusual spring, where we nearly always find something of interest that we had not expected to see. We have found tiny daffodils with heads no bigger than a thumbnail; the graceful white star-like spears of St Bernard's lily; the dramatic tall asphodel of legendary Greek fame; the elegant drooping Solomon's seal, identical to its garden cousin; the low-growing parasitic purple toothwort, tucked low into tree roots on the bank of a stream; dozens of brilliant violets and pansies and a huge variety of more common plants. Anne is now quite used to me suddenly stopping the car and leaping out with the words, "What's that over there?"

I planned one excursion to several churches, ruined chateaux, abbeys and the cloisters at Cadouin. It rained much of the day, but stopped long enough for us to get out of the car to look around at most of our chosen sites without getting absolutely soaked. One turreted chateau was beside a narrow track some miles from the main road. It had been long abandoned, but seemed reasonably sound with its handsome steep *lauze* roof intact. There were extensive ranges of stables, a fine, if weedy courtyard, lovely views and no one else for several miles. It resembled the well-known illustrations from the famous Book of Hours, *'Les trés riches heures du Duc de Berry'*. In the background of several of the twelve incredibly detailed paintings that make up this collection are fantastic castles with fairytale towers, the foregrounds being peopled by rich and poor going about their daily tasks. It needed little imagination to populate this neglected chateau with servants carrying provisions, stable lads shovelling manure, a farm labourer with his pitchfork, the Lord of the Manor arriving on his finely caparisoned horse, the clatter and bustle of a busy working community, and maybe the lady of the house, in elegant finery, sweeping across the cobbles with her scampering children and snuffling hunting dogs.

In contrast, the cloisters at the Cistercian Abbey of Cadouin, also silent, could readily be filled in the imagination with contemplative monks, heads bowed over prayer books, or raised, as ours were, trying to make sense of the multitude of unlikely roof-bosses, each with their message. Complex designs include serene angels and wild beasts, workmen's faces and staring owls, cats or lions, peasants at work and mythological sea creatures In a great dim chapel to one side, displayed in a glass case, is a long, finely-woven linen cloth, embroidered along its borders. This Holy Shroud is believed to be the burial cloth that had been wrapped around Jesus' head and was said

A sculpted cherub

to have been brought to Cadouin from Antioch by a French priest after the First Crusade. Cadouin Monastery was founded in 1115 and shortly afterwards the shroud found its way to the abbey where the monks erected a church in honour of the holy relic. Although Cistercian orders specifically forbade the use of gold, a special dispensation was made for this shroud which was kept safe for a long time in a gold reliquary. Various notables, including Richard the Lionheart and Charles V of France, reverently came on a pilgrimage to pray by it. Simon de Montfort mentioned its existence at the Abbey in 1214, though shortly afterwards Charles VI sent it to Paris where it was exhibited for a month. Then it was sent to Poitiers, which probably saved it from rampaging English soldiers when they overran this area during the turbulent skirmishes of the Hundred Years War.

Edward III had declared himself King of Aquitaine in 1340 and five years later the war began. Soldiers regularly changed sides as one or other of the armies gained the advantage. Land and property were devastated and the wonderfully intricate cloisters at Cadouin were mostly destroyed. Safe from harm, the Shroud was spirited away to monasteries at Toulouse and Aubazine, before returning to its earlier home and present resting place after the country had regained some semblance of peace. It was authenticated by the Church in 1444. The true provenance of this obscure but impressive piece of cloth remains unsure, as the embroidered bands which bear kufic inscriptions have been dated to the 11th century. The cloth itself, however, as far as I know, has not been carbon-dated. Compare the publicity given to the Holy Shroud of Turin, which is considered to be of immense importance to the Catholic community, with this Shroud of Cadouin. Even though modern dating methods have placed the Turin cloth in the late Middle Ages, many believers still devotedly insist on its verity. In their book *The Jesus Conspiracy*, Kersten and Gruber refer to the apocryphal Gospel of the Hebrews, in which a date as early as 335 AD is made for a 'Servant of the Priest' owning the burial shroud, but is that the Turin shroud, or the Cadouin one? The same unnamed person possibly also possessed St Veronica's linen cloth, with its impression of Christ's face (which as I already mentioned may have been brought by her to France), but there is no mention of this head-cloth.

Some treasures have been discovered by pure serendipity. One day, having travelled some distance to see the massive, but bleak and empty, fortified church of St Amand de Coly, we had stopped at the small town of St Geniès to buy some provisions. The church here attracted our attention, as it had many beautifully carved gargoyles and heads, maybe portraits of local people, under the eaves. Gargoyles may have been named after Gargouille, who was a venomous dragon, living in the Seine in the 7th century. He had ravaged the town of Rouen and the Bishop is said to have killed him. Gargouille's memory may be preserved on churches, because here he is forced to do penance by spending eternity spouting water from his mouth, the water symbolising his remorse for the wicked deeds he perpetrated – and so he is attempting to put out the fires he caused in Rouen all those years ago. More prosaically the story could be another allegory for the triumph of Christianity over paganism, like St Michael and the Devil.

So there we were, in St Geniès, browsing in the shop, when we overheard some English tourists asking the way to 'the Chapelle du Cheylard'. Surreptitiously we followed them and were rewarded with a small, disproportionately tall building perched on a smooth grassy mound, just round a corner from the shop. The real surprise was inside, where the walls were smothered with wonderfully well-preserved frescos. A leaflet explained the story behind each of the panels. Clearly visible were St Catherine and her wheel, St Anthony, tempted by devils in the wilderness, and, less familiar, the story of my namesake, St Valérie. A local saint, she was converted to Christianity in the 3rd century by Martial, the first Bishop of Limoges. She steadfastly refused the unwanted attentions of the Duc de Guyenne, and insisted on remaining a virgin. The Duke came into the church in a rage and struck off her head, which she proceeded to pick up. Walking to the altar she presented her disembodied head to the Bishop, who was saying Mass as all this mayhem was going on. Legend goes on to say that the Duke followed her 'step by step' declaring out loud that he had clearly seen angels around his corpse, whereupon he too died. Fanciful or not, this story is pictured in one of the windows of the Cathedral of Limoges. The story was frequently used as the subject for enamel panels of Holy Reliquaries, made in Limoges, in which various saints' fingers, toes or teeth were placed and bought by churches to be honoured by their congregations. A crypt in one of the churches in Limoges contains Valérie's coffin, so even if her story is a fabrication the lady herself seems genuine.

Less happy but very moving was a visit to the site of a wartime atrocity. To the northwest of Limoges lies Oradour-sur-Glane, where one of the most grotesque acts of horror was committed during World War II. One story, which may account for the deaths of 642 people in the village, involves a convoy of unmarked lorries speeding through the area one night, purportedly carrying gold and other treasures stolen by the Germans. They were transporting their booty back to Germany when a resistance group, on their way to blow up a railway, heard the rumbling of the trucks coming fast towards them. The leader of the group ordered his men to stay hidden and not to shoot, but a young enthusiast let fire, at which they were all obliged to follow suit. Most of the soldiers and the resistance fighters were killed. However, one of the *maquis* remained alive and discovering the gold, buried it nearby for later collection. An intriguing book on this story, *'Oradour, Massacre and Aftermath'*, written by Robin Mackness, had far-reaching repercussions, including the imprisonment of its author. He also linked the gold to other, more occult stories in another book, written with Guy Patton, called *'Web of Gold'*. Another possibility is that the murders were done in retribution for the ignominious capture, by the *maquis*, of a senior German officer, who, we are told, was not killed, but released. Whatever the truth of the cause of this brutal massacre, it is indisputable that on 10th June 1944 the SS rounded up everyone in the village, including some youngsters who were just passing through on bicycles. The men were herded into a number of barns where they were machine-gunned and the barns were then set alight. Women and children were locked into the church, which was also burnt. One small boy, a refugee from Lorraine, ran off before the shooting began, as did a few men. One 47-year-old woman threw herself out of a window at the east end of the church and hid among rows of peas in a neighbouring garden until it was all over. A young mother tried to escape with her baby by the same route; they were both killed. The whole village was pillaged and torched. Its stark ruins have been preserved as a memorial. Below ground there is a desperately moving museum of objects excavated from the derelict houses, here a heap of children's toys, there the men's fishing tackle, a pile of melted spectacles. We are not allowed to forget man's inhumanity here.

Some days we are not very lucky with our chosen destinations, but that is the name of the game. In one town, following a lead to a well-publicised church, we had to request the keys from the Mairie. Eventually, down some steps, we found the small door to which the key belonged. Eagerly anticipating a fine interior we were extremely disappointed to find a very bare space, dirty and unfurnished, with broken chairs and discarded chandeliers littering the area behind the altar. We returned the key with a wry smile, wondering why anyone should take the trouble to visit such an unprepossessing place, or to keep it locked. You can't win them all. Another journey in spring, to see daffodils carpeting the fields in the Auvergne, had to be aborted as the road was still blocked with snow. When we travelled many miles into the Aubrac region to see the wolves of Gevaudan – wolves who are free to roam in a large area of forest – the weather unexpectedly turned nasty. We had taken a walk in lovely clear weather before supper in our tiny B&B, which was at the end of a winding, uphill road right off the beaten track. However, in the morning we woke to thick mist and drizzling rain. Not the day to go clambering about in a wolf-filled forest. As soon as we left the area the skies cleared. *C'est la vie!*

But every dive off a main or side road into the rural hinterland may lead to an unexpected pleasure. One such journey took us to the abandoned spa of Salmières. The little road to it, which leads past a lake and a newly-restored restaurant, ended at the dilapidated remains of what must have been quite a smart and fashionable resort in the middle of nowhere. There are no large towns nearby, and there seems to be little publicity about this place, except that put out by the restaurant, which sold small bottles of the water, now extracted commercially from the spring. The bottles are small, so I am informed, as the water has a strong laxative effect. I didn't care to try it.

An advertising leaflet for the restaurant is printed on a reproduction of a faded photograph, which shows a well-populated and fine building, now sad and in the late stages of decay. Some serious effort is being put in to restore the faded elegance of the tiled central structure. A round counter still supports some brass faucets from which the health-giving water would have gushed. Water, within the spa building, is now only supplied by the rain, which penetrates some broken patches of the glass roof. The old photograph shows mostly men (maybe the purgative waters were thought unsuitable for ladies) dressed in three-piece suits, wearing hats. Horses and carriages are bringing more visitors past the lavender and rose-bordered paths. At one side of the path the bandstand still stands, and further on lies the now semi-derelict but imposing guesthouse for those who stayed for several days to take the waters. Let us hope this tasteful restoration continues, though if the restaurant attracts too many people this extraordinary relic of Edwardian style will lose its current magical charm, peopled now only by the ghosts of long departed health-freaks. We walked around the ruined buildings entirely by ourselves, its total seclusion in a remote part of France a secret to all but the most assiduous tourists.

One of the more humorous and zany exhibitions I happened upon was of brightly coloured fish, each about five feet long, mostly made of *objets trouvées* – tools, bits of cars, cogs, nuts and bolts, lumps of unidentifiable metal or wood, partly disguised with fibreglass sheets and all vibrantly painted. One witty model was made of wire, bent into a fish shape and strung about with every kind and size of sardine tin. Other fish, made of tin foil attached to the top of bendy poles, would have made good bird scarers as they flapped and clattered in the breeze. It reminded me of a permanent display of painted and carved sculptures in the garden of an artist at Autoire. The sculptor obviously delights in finding some twisted and tortured chunk of wood in which he can envisage a human form, an animal, or something more fantastic which he then liberates from its prosaic beginnings.

Montpezat-de-Quercy was another of our more spectacular discoveries. The town is pretty, with an arcaded square and picturesque half-timbered and stone buildings, but the church, of simple single-nave structure, held a magnificent treasure. Tapestries, 82 feet in length and 6 feet high were specially woven in the 16th century for the sanctuary. Sixteen sections of the tapestry show the life of St Martin, patron saint of penitent drunkards, to whom the church is dedicated. Their bright colouring and freshness is remarkable, as is the fact that they are still in situ. The detail and clarity of the designs is amazing, making them less tricky to interpret than many murky old tapestries. A man afflicted with spots and pustules is vividly depicted in all his horrible suffering; St Martin's horse is white with blue trappings dangling with tassels; areas of cloth or bits of bodies are outlined with a fine black line, making it all very easy to read. But the story told by the panels is even more important. Martin was obviously a very worthy and charitable man. One story, that has given rise to many paintings, says that in the exceptionally cold winter of 332 he divided his cloak with his sword and gave half to a freezing beggar. Although born to heathen parents in Hungary he became a Christian before he was 15 years old. His father was a Roman soldier and enrolled his son in the cavalry to serve with the army in Gaul. When Martin turned forty, he decided to leave the army, but the Emperor Julian thought that he wanted to quit just to avoid a forthcoming battle. Martin demanded to be allowed to stand naked, with a Cross, in front of the troops during the night before the fight was due to start. In the morning the attackers capitulated and Martin was allowed to leave the army and dedicate his life to religion. In 371 he reluctantly became Bishop of Tours and during this time claims were made that he performed several miracles – including bringing a boy back to life – many of which are represented on the set of tapestries. Later he became a monk at Marmoutiers, from where he would have travelled to preach. He died in November 397 in Touraine and monks from two religious communities raced to collect his body. His relics would have been of great value. The monks from his own monastery won and reported that on the return journey trees burst into leaf and flowers bloomed. Miracles continued to surround his tomb and he became the first saint who had not been martyred. In fact he is remembered forever in the word 'chapel'. His cloak was known as a 'cappella' (Italian for chapel). The word later came to denote a mobile shrine containing part of his cloak. Later it came to mean a permanent sanctuary in a church, where relics, visited by pilgrims, would be housed, hence all the radiating chapels behind the high altars of many churches.

Churches, abbeys, chateaux, caves, sculpture, art, history, mystery, magic, nature, scenery; any one of these or several may be the objective of one of our days out. It is the chance of encountering some strange and mysterious piece of local history, or a craftsman's bizarre imagination that excites Anne and me on our journeys. We love our 'adventures' and avidly search articles and books for new places to go. It is incredible how often we come up with some suggestion for a trip to somewhere really thrilling that has been virtually passed over in a guide book or magazine.

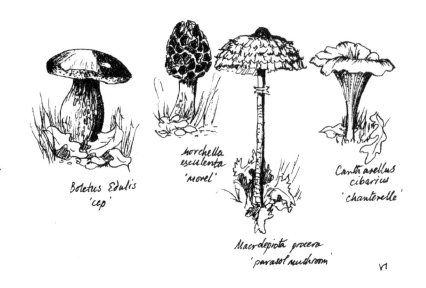

Boletus Edulis
'cep'

Morchella
esculenta
'morel'

Cantharellus
cibarius
'chanterelle'

Macrolepiota procera
'parasol mushroom'

vi

Chapter 11

FOOD, WONDERFUL FOOD

France is blessed with a diverse climate capable of sustaining a variety of abundant crops. Of great importance in our particular area are strawberries, which are in season from Easter to October. Beaulieu hosts an annual and highly popular Strawberry Fair in May, when the whole town is decorated with bunting and dedicates itself wholeheartedly to the festivities. The council has even erected permanent ugly, large metal signs, at either end of the town, advertising its affinity with the strawberry. Each year there is a new theme to the town celebrations. A huge fibreglass cornucopia was erected one year, spilling vast amounts of succulent strawberries onto the ground. What a waste! One of the *boulangeries* bakes a world-record breaking tart, some 24 feet across, which is exhibited in the main square and then sold to thousands of greedy visitors.

Half a ton of ingredients is used for the dough and 800 kilos of strawberries. Most of the region's market gardeners set up elaborately decorated stalls to sell the many types of strawberries available, including the long-fruited and superbly sweet *gariguette*, one of the earliest and tastiest varieties. It is almost overwhelmingly tempting to buy punnets of each, to compare the subtle, differing tastes. A serious allergic reaction would probably result from indulging this desire, as there are round small strawberries, round large ones, dark red, bright red, long ones... all wafting a heady, if sickly aroma into the air.

Musicians and dancers, some from the Auvergne, entertain the crowds with old-style set dances with dainty steps, accompanied by fascinating folk music. Instruments include small but loud bagpipes, common throughout the world where goats or sheep abound as their skins are used for the air bags. These bagpipes from central France do not have a mouth-blown pipe to fill the skins with air, as in Scotland; instead, the red cloth-covered bags have a leather valve, which controls the flow of air, and is activated by the player using his left arm to squeeze and release the bellows strapped to his chest. All this elbow action continues rhythmically, while the performer fingers the recorder-style pipe to produce the tune. A fiddle, a small button-accordion and a very decorative hurdy-gurdy add their wheezy, piercing tones, best suited to the open air. Hurdy-gurdys are strange objects, which seem like a hotchpotch of bits and pieces of other instruments put together at random. The body is like a stumpy lute, with a set of strings. On top of that is a construction similar to half a barrel with keys looking like a doctor's tongue spatula, which are depressed onto the strings to change their length, and thereby the pitch. At one end is a handle, which is constantly turned to activate a set of hidden strings which sound together, much as the background drone-sounds of the bagpipes. Amazingly these complicated instruments have been known since the 8th century; they are a precursor to the spinet and therefore the piano! The musicians I saw at the strawberry fair were fetchingly dressed in traditional costume; the men, in white shirts, black trousers and waist-coats wore wide-brimmed, shallow-crowned, felt hats and the ladies were in long dresses, aprons, thick white stockings, black shoes, paisley shawls and straw hats tied on with ribbons over lace-edged bonnets.

Sweet chestnut trees grow in profusion on the hillsides. The nuts, when dried and crushed, make a flour which was used in years gone by as a cheap alternative to wheat flour. It makes a solid bread, but used with sugar, spices and eggs as a tart filling it is very pleasant. In the autumn the *boulangeries* still make cakes with chestnut flour, and also sell sweets packaged in appropriate *papier maché* containers designed like splitting green chestnut husks showing their shiny nuts inside.

Beaulieu's surrounding countryside is home to thousands of walnut trees, whose leaves appear late in spring. They often seem dead, with their gnarled twigs and deeply textured trunks frequently coated with dark mosses. But the crop is one of the most important financially for the farmers as a range of unlikely foods and drinks is made from the nuts, and even from their leaves. Heady, scented and richly flavoured oil, used mainly for salad dressings, has been milled for centuries. Many old mills are still functioning and the current interest in gour-met food has ensured not just their survival but the construc-tion of new factories, which also produce walnut vinegar, so full of flavour that on salad it makes a good dieter's alternative to oil. Crushed or ground nuts are added to honey or choco-late, for delicious fattening treats. What with all the jam made at the Andros factory, who produce the well-known Bonne Maman brand, just down the road at Biars, one wonders when the French eat these sweet spreads, other than for breakfast, as they've never taken to 'teatime'. Anyway an appropriately named local firm, Denoix ('of nuts') distils wines and liqueurs from the whole nuts, together with their unripe green casings, and also a thick strong aperitif from the leaves. Heavy coarse breads, crunchy with broken walnuts, are marvellous with cheese for lunch, and flans and cakes make use of the crushed kernels. Market traders often offer tempting samples of these flattish, close-textured cakes to entice passers-by to purchase.

In the kitchen at La Folie Verte there is a heap of walnuts in a shallow dish, alongside two rocks, one large with an indentation, the other fitting neatly into the palm of the hand. Cracking the shells using the rocks is an efficient method of ensuring that nine times out of ten the nuts emerge whole and uncrushed. This bizarre ritual dates to a holiday in Morocco when, together with some friends, we travelled over the Tizi and Test pass from Taroudant to Marrakesh. At the top of the pass we were delighted to find a small simple restaurant, where we stopped for lunch of omelettes, salad and water (this being a Muslim country). As each omelette was prepared and served separately it all took a long time. We sat at a table beside the road with amazing views. In one direction we looked back down the steep road with its multitude of hairpin bends to the heat-lashed desert floor and the distant haze of the Taroudant oasis, and in the other we faced the snow-tipped peaks of the Atlas Mountains. This phenomenal panorama made the wait a pleasure. When the omelettes and salad were cleared away our host brought a large dish of walnuts. As we had no shared language we gesticulated that we had a problem. How could we open the walnuts without a nutcracker? The restaurateur silently went to the side of the road, picked up two suitable rocks and demonstrated the simple method we have used ever since.

At least 365 cheeses are made in France, so we are informed, most of which I have never come across. The Limousin cow's milk is used for a number of superb cheeses. A creamy, round slab, sold on squares of waxed paper in the nearby supermarket, goes particularly well with the local walnuts. Several wonderful smooth blue cheeses come from the region: Bleu d'Auvergne, Bleu d'Aurillac, and Fourme d'Ambert to name but a few, which makes choosing very difficult. Farmhouse St Nectaire and the vast and varied Cantal cheeses, the nearest thing to a cheddar, are usually on our shopping list. Sheep-milk cheese, either soft or semi-hard, is sold as *'brebis'*, meaning 'ewe'. (I had mistakenly thought that *'mouton'* was the right name for a sheep but I found out that it means either the male sheep or mutton). These cheeses are a delicious treat – they are usually quite expensive since ewes don't produce much milk. Then there are the little round goat cheeses, predominantly the *'cabecou'*, which traditionally comes from Rocamadour. Fresh with a salad, or grilled as a starter on a bed of lettuce, drizzled with walnut oil, *cabecou* is delicious. In its ageing state, brown and smelly, I find it quite unacceptable, though it is a highly-prized local delicacy.

I was equally unimpressed with of a dish of snails, prepared by one of my friends. Jenny is a superb cook and has an amazing gift for creating something delicious out of nothing much, or random leftovers, but her efforts to be super-economical and make something out of the snails in the garden were somewhat less appealing. I have never been very fond of snails. They are too similar to their disgusting cousins, slugs, of which we have a proliferation of enormous rust coloured ones, sometimes five inches long, in the garden at Folie. Admittedly the snails in question were the edible Roman ones, *Helix pomatia*, but Jenny was not prepared to be patient enough to prepare them properly. They have to be fed on lettuce for about a week, to ensure that all poisons they may have absorbed from plants are cleared from their systems, but after only a day or two she decided to cook them. She even offered some to our elderly neighbour next door, who, I hope, had the sense to throw them away. I had a distinctly runny tummy the following day, though Jenny never owned up to any adverse reaction.

Much more successful have been my fungi forays. Over the years I have learned to recognise a number of edible varieties. Another friend, Geraldine, insisted on photographing the moment I crawled beneath a barbed wire fence to liberate a particularly fine specimen of Parasol mushroom, *macrolepiota procera*, a tall fringed mushroom with a stem patterned like snakeskin. Its immature young look like drumsticks. The woods surrounding our valley are prime fungi-hunting grounds, with oak, beech and chestnut trees, damp, with scattered sunlit open spaces. I have found the inedible-looking *cep*, or penny bun mushroom, on a few occasions. It looks very unappetising with its sticky brown cap and greenish-yellow spongelike tubes in place of gills, but it is one of the finest to eat, and often appears in local restaurants in indecently rich dishes accompanying duck and goose. Packets of dried *ceps* were good presents to bring home, until they became readily available in English supermarkets. In France, indeed in most countries on the continent, chemists display posters in their windows, illustrating edible and poisonous mushrooms and are obliged to identify any specimens brought to them. Few edible varieties are sold in the markets in France. In Hungary, however, I have seen tables in the market, laden with an amazing array of rare wild mushrooms, each bearing a certificate from the authorities guaranteeing its safety. The dangerous ones are also laid out, with warnings as to their toxicity. It is all too easy to mis-identify fungi, and many deaths occur every year as a result. I think it unlikely anyone would mistake *boletus edulis*, the *cep*, for *boletus satanus*, with its red tubes, white cap and swollen red stem, which, if eaten, may not be a certain killer but would make you very sick. One stinking fungus, which I had trouble identifying, looked like a hand-sized red starfish. I found it on a walk with friends and one of them bravely carried it back to the house on a large leaf. It was not mentioned in my reference books and it took a visit to a more erudite bookshop – one in Cambridge – to find an illustration of this odd fungus. I now know it to be a *clathrus archeri*, apparently not terribly uncommon, though I have never found another, before or since.

Another mushroom, which does not have instant plate-appeal – or name-appeal – is the *trompette de mort*, though its common name is *'la viande des pauvres,'* 'meat of the poor.' Its English name, 'horn of plenty' is more pleasing and it is fairly easy to find among oak-leaf litter. Less common, but some-

Houses by the riverside at Argentat

times found in the greengrocer's shop in Beaulieu, are
chanterelles, sometimes called *girolles*, orange-coloured and del-
icately smelling of dried apricots. They remind me of the water
towers visible all over France, which have a narrow stem-like
supporting pillar and then curving ribs holding up the flat-
topped cistern, except that the top of the fungus is wavy and
indented. *Chanterelles* are wonderful in omelettes or made into
soup. I have never had the good fortune to find *morels*, which
look like small, brownish, wrinkled brains. Neither have I
found any *pied de mouton*, another water tower designer's
influence? Again, I have only seen these for sale on rare
occasions. White and firm of flesh, its distinguishing characteristic is the underside of its cap, which resembles tiny stalactites. Whether sheep's feet are in any way textured like this I
have never discovered. Field and horse mushrooms are quite
common, though difficult to gather as they tend to grow in private meadows rather than woods. Even the woods are usually
private and trespass notices warning that '*Chasse de
Champignons Interdit*' are common. I was once given half of a
giant puffball, which was memorable only for its prodigious
capacity to soak up a gross amount of butter. It seems that the
English have lost interest in collecting wild mushrooms, which
are just as plentiful as in France. One does, however, hear of the
team, mostly composed of mid-European immigrants, who
know what to look for and where, who gather quantities of
fungi from Surrey woods for Antonio Carluccio's shops and
restaurant.

Foie gras is a traditional local product. It is as well not to visit
a goose or duck farm if you are squeamish about the way the
birds are fed. The birds, once caught, are held by the neck, a
long funnel inserted and the corn poured down, helped on its
way by a sort of winding mechanism, like a 'Moulimix' used
for purées. Farmers claim that the birds do not mind at all
being force-fed with good grain to swell their livers in order to
produce this glorious dish. Recently I have been served with
an unusual *pâté de foie gras*, layered with sliced figs. Sarlat mar-

ket is the place to buy fresh *foie* or blocks of ready-to-serve *mi-cuit* goose or duck liver. The fresh livers are pale and flaccid, and should be thinly sliced before flash-frying in a little butter. Monbazillac is usually recommended to be drunk with *foie gras*, which seems inappropriate as it is sweet, but surprisingly it complements the rich flavour of the meat. Recently I have discovered a much rarer and very local wine called Vin Paillé, which is also excellent with *foie gras*. This sweet wine has something of the characteristics of German *eiswein*, where the grapes are left on the vine until frost breaks down their inner structure. With Vin Paillé, the grapes are cut and laid on beds of straw to allow them to dry out, almost like raisins, thereby concentrating the flavour. Afterwards the grapes are pressed to create a small output of heavenly golden wine, similar to a muscatel but drier, which is a good accompaniment for desserts as well.

The valley between Beaulieu and Argentat used to be a great area for vineyards, but after the devastation that phylloxera brought about at the turn of the 20th century, few vines remain. Within a few miles from us, the Côtes de Glanes co-operative produced an award-winning red wine in 2000, and a good fresh summer *rosé*. Mille et Une Pierres, from vineyards near Meyssac, is another acceptable *vin du pays*, which improves on keeping for a few years. Otherwise, tiny remnants of the old vineyards used by the local residents for making their own wine survive on the sloping sides of our part of the valley. Legal limits exist for the amount of wine that can be made by an individual, and rules also control the making of fruit spirits. At Collonges la Rouge I have seen a travelling still, or *alambic*, complex in design, with copper tubes, tanks and pipes, used for turning plums or strawberries, or whatever fruit is available, into fiery flavoured *eau de vie*. Sadly these skills will soon be lost, as the Government has decreed that existing licences to produce spirits will expire with their present owners and cannot be passed on to sons or other family.

Unflavoured *eau de vie* is also sold commercially, for making very alcoholic fruit infusions. A friend who stayed in a B&B in the blackcurrant-growing region of France was given the landlady's recipe for *Crème de Cassis*, which he passed on to me. As I grow huge quantities of blackcurrants in England, this seemed an excellent way of using them up.

To one kilo of fruit add one litre of red wine (nothing special). Crush the berries a little with a potato masher and leave the mixture for 24 hours. Strain off the liquid. To each litre of juice add one kilo of sugar and bring gently to the boil. Boil for six minutes. Use one wineglass of *eau de vie* per bottle and top up with the sugary, winey, blackcurrant juice. Cork the bottles for storage. The *Crème de Cassis* is immediately ready for use. A tablespoon or two in the bottom of a glass, topped with a light white wine (or champagne if you are feeling flush) makes the wonderful apéritif, Kir, named after a Monsieur Kir, mayor of a town which produced too many blackcurrants. He invented this drink and kept everyone happy.

Eau de vie can also be used to make drinks like English sloe gin, but it's much cheaper. Wild plums, sometimes called bullace, make a potent drink like slivovitz. Slash each plum with a knife and pile them into screw-top jars, about two-thirds full. Add two or three large tablespoons of sugar and top up with *eau de vie*. Seal the tops of the jars and hide in a dark cupboard until you gleefully rediscover them two or three years later. Amaze your friends with a home-made hooch that both tastes fantastic and is extremely (almost dangerously) powerful.

To enjoy the best of Corezzienne cuisine, one must regularly sample the menus of the local restaurants. None, in our vicinity, boasts a Michelin star. However, trial and error, practice and recommendations have led us to a number of excellent establishments. I hesitate to mention any by name, as this may lead to their popularity being so great that either they would change their character or it would become impossible to book a table less than a month in advance, as has happened to some highly-rated restaurants in Lyons and the South of France. Suffice it to say that there are outstanding meals at reasonable prices to be had almost wherever you look. At one nearby Relais des Routiers, we had chosen a four-course meal for about £9.50. Having ordered, Madame asked if we would like soup.

"Soup?" we said, not seeing it on the menu.

"Soup!" she replied, so, mystified, we agreed. A great tureen was plonked, without ceremony, onto the table for us to help ourselves. It was not on the bill. Neither was there any limit to the amount of *terrine* we could have heaped onto our plates. There is a difference between a gourmand (and on this occasion, we were exactly that, greedy and gluttonous) and a gourmet, who loves fine food and wines and probably eats them in delicate moderation. We have one favourite restaurant, perched on a hillside about 15 miles south of us. Not only is the food exquisite, but the view from its flower-filled dining terrace, on a sunny evening when there are just a few clouds, is wonderful. Across the increasingly darkening valleys and small undulating hills you can watch the sun setting in the furthest distance, lighting up the streaky sky with all colours of red and gold. One evening my eye was drawn to the gourmet menu, seven courses, including lobster, at about £37. Every course was perfection and carefully balanced. At the end of the evening, as each course wasn't too large, I was not over-stuffed but just pleasantly full, having experienced some of the very best of French cooking.

Highlights on local menus include *salade correzienne*, a mound of green salad sprinkled with walnuts, thin slices of smoked duck breast, sometimes a little *foie gras*, croutons, walnut oil and *gesiers* (preserved duck gizzards). This last ingredient probably wouldn't appeal to all, but the method of preparing them, like the twice-cooked *confits*, renders them tasty and tender. Don't miss it. Little trout from the Dordogne or Cère are often served, as in England, with almonds, as a second course. Then comes the meat, which is, as often as not, duck, as a *confit* or the *magret* (breast) served just pink. Sometimes steak, with a sauce of *ceps* or *morels* will be offered, frequently with a timbale of rice and a small mound of vegetable purée, celeriac or turnip. Some special delicacy may be flavoured with truffles, those extravagant, earthy lumps of fungus found traditionally in oak woods by pigs. Now, more often, dogs are used for the hunt as they are less partial to the buried treasure and are therefore less likely to gobble them up before the hunter can rescue them. Apparently tiny midges hover a few feet off the ground under which you might be fortunate enough to find truffles, but as they mostly grow to the west of the Corrèze, a find is unlikely. To follow there is the cheese board, with at least four local cheeses, and then desserts... nutty ice-creams, tarts of apple, pear, nuts again or apricot, a mousse, *iles flottants* (just what this 'Tigger' doesn't like), or sometimes the superb fondant of chocolate. I searched high and low for this recipe, which I have eventually found. The pudding is baked in a *bain marie*. Its texture is a bit like a firm sponge, but when the middle is cut open, hot, runny chocolate pours out of it. To hell with the diet!

Simple lunches in the garden are the way we, as a family, most appreciate French food. I usually start the week with a leisurely morning shopping in Beaulieu, gathering the ingredients for several days of pleasurable eating. My first job after a cup of coffee, back at home, is to start a *potage* or *garbure* – good word, that. Onions, leek, celery, potatoes and carrots are the main ingredients, all roughly chopped, thrown into water to cover and simmered with a few chicken stock cubes, pepper, salt and herbs until the vegetables are all soft. Then with the hand-held whizzer I purée the whole thing to a thick tasty mush. Lunch is a bowl of this soup, with a crusty baguette or walnut bread, followed by a variety of cheeses, *pâtés* and a salad of tomatoes and lettuce sprinkled with a little walnut oil, maybe some grated celeriac or carrot in a vinaigrette dressing, then some fresh fruit, hopefully peaches or strawberries, and a handful of walnuts, all washed down with a glass or two of local plonk. What more could one ask for? Friends always comment that they should eat like this at home, whereupon we reply that we do, frequently, but it's never quite the same. The bread is never so fresh, nor the salad, unless it has come out of the kitchen garden. The *pâtés* are not home-made by the butcher, and the cheeses rarely at the point of perfection. You are often asked, when purchasing a soft cheese or a melon, on which day it is to be eaten, to be sure of the exact ripeness at the right moment.

Dinner, if not eaten out, is also usually a simple meal. We might have a golden corn-fed chicken, or some lamb grilled on the cast-iron skillet, flavoured with fresh rosemary from the bush by the steps, new potatoes boiled with some of the apple-mint that grows wild all over the garden, green beans, or earthy carrots, sold with their greenery still attached. Even easier to cook in the microwave are portions of the *'plat du jour'* each butcher prepares fresh each day. Often there is a choice of two or three dishes such as *coq au vin* or rabbit with mushrooms.

What you cannot expect, generally, in France is a wide variety of imported foreign foods. Nearly everything in the green-grocer's or the supermarkets is French. Oranges, lemons and bananas are available, but pineapples, mangoes and other exotic fruits are rarely on the shelves. Vegetables are those in season – not expensive and often under-ripe imports from South Africa or Kenya as we might find in our own supermarkets. You eat produce unpolluted by radiation, with dirt on the celery and potatoes, and you must accept variations in the shape or size of the sweet bulbous Mediterranean tomatoes. Natural, delicious food.

Chapter 12

NATURE IN THE RAW

France hosts a number of animals, rare if not unknown in England, and La Folie Verte appears to have become home to a wide variety of them. Initially we had to deal with occasional rats and mice, inevitable as they are attracted to the rabbits and rabbit food which my neighbour keeps close to my back wall. Poison has to be put down regularly. We did buy a device which emits a high-pitched bleep meant to deter them but it doesn't seem to do any good at all – they either like the sound or are totally deaf. A friend of Pippa, staying with us for a few days, was on his way to bed when he called out, " Pippa, I think there's a mouse on the stairs."

"No, Morgan," she said calmly when she saw the little furry beast, "that's a rat! Mummy, there's a rat on the stairs."

I quickly grabbed the garden rake and rushed to where the

two of them were still guarding the small creature, and with a forceful thrust, struck the rat as hard as I could. As I removed the rake the injured animal ran past us all and disappeared down a hole in the floorboards. To be quite sure that it wouldn't emerge from the same hole, I jammed some stones from the garden into the hole, and then plastered it over with Polyfilla. We then went to bed.

While chatting to my neighbours, the Clouseaus, about the problems of dealing with pests, they told me a story about some work they had had done in their loft. Several whole chickens' eggs were lying on the floor. No doubt old and bad, but complete and not eaten. What animal steals eggs, has the capacity in its mouth for a hen's egg, but doesn't have the ability or desire to break into it?

One night, Tony and I were woken by the sound of something trying to saw through the ceiling – at least that was our impression at two or three in the morning. Rationalising the terrifying experience the next day, we surmised that squirrels had taken walnuts into the gap between the floor and the ceiling and were attempting to eat them. However, I later found out it was probably something else. Neatly laid out on a fallen tile in one of the bedrooms were some dried-up, finger-sized odourless droppings. Some months afterwards, while talking in the garden to Pierre, the man who cuts my grass, he indicated a cluster of similar droppings on the grass.

"*Ah. Vous avez les martres!*" he declared.

"*Qu'est ce que c'est, les martres?*" I enquired, upon which there followed a comical description of the unknown animals. Pierre intimated, with precise gestures that it was something about 18 inches long. His hands then undulated through the air, leading me to realise that we were entertaining animals from the weasel family. Apparently they frequently colonise lofts by climbing up rough walls or leaping onto the roof from nearby trees. Being destructive pests they are often shot or trapped. Two similar creatures exist, the *martre*, or marten (pine marten) and the *fouine* (stone marten). Both have honey-brown coats, the *martre* being paler with a yellow patch under the throat. The patch on the *fouine* is white. We still hear them vigorously romping around upstairs at night and scampering over the lean-to roof, but I have never seen one. I have laid traps, put down poison and thumped the ceiling with a broom handle at night... all to no avail. They obviously like our loft – or our company.

Unpleasant and destructive are loft-based communities of smaller invaders – beetles. Apart from ordinary woodworm and the large wood-boring beetles which live in the rafters, there are harmless but stinky shield beetles, so-called because of the shape of their wing-cases. If crushed they give off a foul bitter almond odour, which is quite persistent. Like skunks they can react if they are merely disturbed, so it's difficult to get rid of them without causing a nasty smell. Flipped onto a piece of paper and quickly dropped out of the windows is my preferred method. I also often find their dead and desiccated bodies lying around upstairs. What they are doing indoors at all mystifies me as my books tell me they are meant to live in trees.

More worrying was a sound heard above the ceiling in the loft bedrooms, where the spaces between the rafters are lined with polystyrene-backed plasterboard. Rubbing your palms up and down with dry hands produces a comparable sound to the one I could hear. We had snakes! Grass snakes, I was informed, who enjoy the warmth and dryness under roofs, but unnerving to hear them rustling over your head all the same. The house was full, apart from one of these loft bedrooms when Pippa arrived one year. I didn't say anything, but she came down to breakfast, having had a bad night's sleep, saying that she would sleep in the living room for the rest of her holiday as she'd heard noises above her. I had to admit to knowing the reason for her disturbed sleep. Obtaining some noxious liquid, which I had been assured would *'dissuader les serpents'* from the local hardware shop, I sprayed the smelly stuff around the walls inside and out. It seemed to work, since when Lulu arrived a day or so later and was put in the same bedroom, she made no comment about unearthly noises in the night. We didn't immediately tell her why Pippa had vacated the room but she later cheerfully mentioned that she had found a dead snake in the same room the previous year. Guests had also seen one of these enormous *couleuvres* which grow to twice the length of English grass snakes. It had fallen off the oil store roof and terrified the visiting lady, who ran screaming down the road to where her husband and child were talking to the local shepherd. He rushed to the house with the family, and then declared that it was *"Pas méchant, pas méchant"* (not dangerous) and promptly killed it with his crook! The only visible sign I have ever found of these unwanted visitors is a length of papery shed skin trapped in the rough stones of the garden wall. I've now made sure that the *maçon* has sealed every hole in the stone walls of the loft where a snake could get in. Vipers also live in our part of the world, though they prefer warm damp places like compost heaps and neglected gardens, but I haven't encountered any of those yet. My neighbours obviously have, since they warned me of the danger of cutting long grass, or hacking at the invasive thicket of bamboo which my predecessor cursed me with, without wearing long wellington boots and protective clothing.

One year we were troubled by an invasion of hornets nesting in the walls of the house. In France the *sappeurs-pompiers* or firemen deal with these sorts of problems. They arrived promptly, when called, and the one who was to climb the ladder proceeded to don a white, all-enveloping spacesuit, gloves and helmet. Slowly, because it was obviously difficult to move any faster, he approached the hole where they were coming and going and squirted some foam at high pressure into it. Then the *pompiers* told me they really had no idea where the hornets might be, as they had probably travelled some distance from the outside through small gaps between the stones, so the chemical was unlikely to have killed the nest. Assuring me that hornets and wasps almost never return to the same site another year, the *pompiers* disrobed and left. Fortunately hornets fly quite slowly, so those managing to get into the house are very easy to swat or spray. Sadly, that same year our friendly shepherd was stung in the crook of the elbow by a vicious hornet and died only half an hour later. Possibly he died of shock, or maybe because the poison had such a short distance to travel to the heart.

The grass (or rather the weeds) is constantly disturbed by yet more unwelcome guests. Moles. The soft bare mounds they throw up litter the garden. One mole can form three or four heaps a day in our beautifully friable earth, and though they rarely uproot any plants that matter, they make the garden look unkempt and the so-called lawn ripples with so many humps and bumps that even walking becomes an obstacle course. I have tried putting poison into their runs, but there are so many, it is difficult to find them all. Observers might have wondered what strange ritual I was conducting, as I walked in circles around every molehill, testing the ground for evidence of a soft patch. On finding one I stuck a thick pole into the ground, penetrating the moles' tunnels and spooned in some of the toxic granules I had bought. Hopefully, the disruption we'll cause by building the swimming pool might send them somewhere quieter, like the neighbour's chicken run.

The visiting cats never seem to catch moles, though I have seen the remains of mice left as a present by Mignon, one of a pair of sweet-natured, though shy, black and white cats who used to live next door. Her brother was, one hopes mistakenly, shot by a local hunter, and Mignon lasted another 12 years before succumbing to a throat tumour. I still miss her a lot. She would often call in for some milk when I was there, though some of my guests never saw her at all. Her best trick was to leap for the handle of the French door to the kitchen, which she pulled down if she could hang on long enough. Sometimes she just heaved her shoulder at the door, making it rattle, until I opened it for her. Chicken or fish scraps were eagerly devoured, though always with one eye on the door – just in case I closed it. She was definitely frightened of being shut in. Other feline visitors have come and gone, strays I suppose: a lovely friendly tabby and white, a ginger tom and one who belonged to villagers down the hill, a half-Siamese, with crossed blue eyes, a very flat face and a mischievous temperament. All are made welcome at Folie, if for nothing else than to chase away or kill vermin.

What we do not welcome are flies, mosquitoes and wasps, which we attempt to discourage with a hanging, flying insect destroyer which glows a livid blue. It frequently attracts moths, however, which fizz and crackle as their wings beat against the hot wires. When Pippa came with a group of her friends one summer, they devised a competition whereby they scored points for every fly they killed; one for a fly, five for a wasp, ten for a horse fly and minus ten for a bee. Apparently flies take off backwards, but it still needs very fast reactions to trap them. I did eventually have to ban the game at the dinner table, as the dishes rattled unnervingly with every smack of a hand on the table. Pippa claimed that one of her friends cheated by standing on an apple with several wasps on it. Anyway, they each scored over 100 points and were possibly more efficient pest destroyers than those awful, old-fashioned fly papers – gruesome, sticky killing grounds.

Guests, who are asked to write whatever they like in the Visitors' Book, most often complain of the cockerel who noisily commands his harem of hens in the neighbour's chicken-run. I truly never hear him in the early morning, but other visitors, perhaps more used to town noise, find their sleep regularly broken by his raucous dawn greetings. What I do hear is the comforting sound of the church bells in the village, which are rung – or nowadays, are set off by an automatic timer – at eight in the morning, then again at noon and at seven in the evening. Presumably the bells were originally used to mark important times for prayers. It is possible that the early bell was for Lauds, that at midday for the Angelus and the one at seven for Vespers, though the French refer to the 'Angelus du *matin, du midi et du soir'*, so maybe the same prayer was said three times a day. Listening to these tintinabulations in the rosy light of a warm evening reminds me of the painting called 'The Angelus' by Millet. Two pious peasants stand in a furrowed field, heads bowed, hands together, beside their wheelbarrow, which is loaded with a basket and a long-handled fork and sacks, perhaps full of potatoes. The sky is pink in the fading evening light and in the far distance, on the horizon, is a church. This, Millet's most famous painting, exhibited in Paris in 1859, was a gift to The Louvre from a benefactor who had paid 800,000 francs to its American owner for it; a far cry from the original sum of 1,500 francs which Millet received. Millet lived and worked with a group of high-minded and often religious painters at Barbizon, near Fontainbleau. Gustave Courbet, whose one-man show in a shack in Paris was called *'Le Réalisme'*, was perhaps the most well-known and revolutionary of the members. Their subjects were frequently the peasants seen around the village, and they believed in representing truth, not prettiness. However, perhaps their subjects did not appeal to the bourgeoisie of the time, as, on Millet's death, his widow had to ask the state for a miserable pension of 1,200 francs... But then maybe the bells are nothing to do with religion at all, and are more prosaically indications of the times when farmers should go to work, for lunch and at the end of the day. Note that there is no bell to tell the workers to go back to work after lunch. Long live the long lunch hour, or two.

Comments about spiders of all sizes are also frequently written in the guest book – understandable, as we have many of the type whose long legs are almost invisibly thin, dangling from every corner and beam, when no one has whisked them away. And the fat hairy ones we all hate in our baths also appear from time to time. Martine, my cleaner, bravely battles with their insistent repopulation each time she comes, but inevitably their militant advance is impossible to overcome totally. Country dwellers have to get used to sharing their living space with all varieties of small and large wildlife. The thing that really gives me the creeps, which I occasionally see skittering up the wall, is a kind of thin centipede, *lithobius for-ficatus*, with extremely long legs, which has the nasty habit of feeding on its own young. These two-inch russet-coloured intruders I will not tolerate, and rarely miss with a well-aimed sole of a shoe or rolled up paper, even though they try to scuttle away into dark hidey-holes.

In the garden and on countryside walks, more acceptable wildlife scampers and flutters around our feet and heads. Multicoloured butterflies delight in the honey-scented flowers of the buddleia. Silver-washed fritillaries, peacocks, white and purple emperors, red admirals, acid-yellow brimstones, warm-toned clouded yellows, almost extinct in England, swallow-tails, and the extraordinary false swallowtails, which appear to be flying backwards, as their wings point sharply forwards, are all regular visitors. Harmless hummingbird hawkmoths, which can easily be confused with hornets, speedily whirr their wings into a blur while extending their curved probosces deep into the purple tunnels of the buddleia florets. Elsewhere there are multitudes of unidentified 'little brown jobs', proba-bly wood browns, skippers and commas, and beautiful dainty blues. Among everyday weeds, like nettles and dandelions ('*piss-en-lit*', in French, because of the diuretic effect of its milky sap), flit the dramatic Arctia caja, or Garden tiger moths (no, not the old biplanes). They are among the limited number of moths which mainly fly in sunshine, showing off their brilliant orange and black spotted underwings and black and white wavy-striped upper wings, which contrast in a way no interi-or designer would dare to combine.

The Visitors' Book was used by one enthusiastic group of birdwatchers to list all the species they saw, both in the garden and around the district. I have seen many of the fifty or so types that they listed, including the black redstart with its black chest, grey back and shocking scarlet tail. Pied and spot-ted flycatchers perch briefly on the telegraph wires, poised to swoop and dive for their minute prey. Red and black kites are fearsome hunters of unwary rabbits, voles and mice. To watch these magnificent birds of prey swoop from a great height, plunging to earth in one smooth curve is a rare and splendid sight. Buzzards, usually in pairs, are quite prolific, and can be seen and heard wheeling and crying over our house most days, or sitting hunched over their quarry in the fields or on fence posts beside the road. However, I have never seen a golden oriole, a yellow relation of the blackbird, which my twitchers had spotted. I am very envious. Anne and I once heard one calling, when we were walking in a remote corner of the Corrèze. I remain in hope of a sighting one day.

We are far enough south for lots of lizards, both small, brown and common and the less familiar, large emerald green ones with turquoise heads, who run over terraces and up walls all day long. One night, returning home from supper with Anne, I was startled to pick out something far stranger in my headlights, just down the road from my house. I left the car, headlights blazing, in the middle of the deserted road and rushed in for my camera. Sitting quite still on the road were two fire salamanders, lumpy lizards about eight inches in length, black and blotched with vivid yellow spots and patches. They stayed long enough for their portraits to be taken and then ambled off into the grass. I had never even heard of such things.

You'd imagine that wild rabbits and deer would be as common in France as in England. Either they never quite took such a firm hold, or the hunters are more efficient, but there do not seem to be as many in France. Wild boar sound as if they would be more exciting to hunt. Anne recalled a day when she was walking in some woods when what had appeared to be a heap of stones suddenly got up and started to trot away. The little 'marcassins,' as the baby boars are called, look quite different from their brown, hairy, sharp-toothed and dangerous parents. Their coats are striped – effective camouflage in the patchy light and shade of the woods. Sows are known to defend their young ferociously if they feel threatened, and the males will attack without any provocation, so Anne made a measured but hasty retreat to safety.

Red squirrels are a common sight, frolicking among the trees on the hillside above our house. They are not really red at all, but dark russet-brown, almost black at times. As grey squirrels have not yet migrated to this area the smaller, more delicate red squirrels are thriving. It is hard to view them as tree rats; they are too pretty. Regrettably the only times we have seen badgers they have been dead, lying beside the road, their foul odour filling the air long before the body is in view. They are surprisingly large animals, but being mainly nocturnal you're unlikely to catch sight of them very often. I do, however, remember my first ever view of one, boldly crossing a bare field in Surrey, while I was on the bus going to school. I wanted to tell everyone on the bus to look to their left, but was too shy in those days.

Aural senses are frequently assaulted with the incessant chatter of grasshoppers when the weather is warm. They are often joined by the raucous grating of solitary and invisible *cicadas* who disguise themselves as bits of bark while calling for a mate. Sitting by the river at our favourite bathing place, the air is usually full of the dongs and clangs of cowbells from a herd of Limousin cattle on the other bank. The sound reminds me of the school bells of my childhood but the urge to jump up and get in line has thankfully left me now.

Nature affects us weather-wise too. The area is 50 miles or so from the Auvergne, where the predominantly west winds often blow in heavy rain clouds. This accounts for the eternal greenness of the Dordogne, so different from the bleached and parched southern hills of Provence. In summer the air is heavy with humidity, growing overwhelming, until the almost predictable fortnightly thunderstorms we love to watch crashing round the valley finally freshen the stultified air. After storms the grateful dwellers in the hot loft rooms can at last get a good night's sleep. Sometimes at night, when storms surround us, the ring of hills is completely lit up, red, green, purple and white, like transient floodlights. The torrential rain lashes down vertically or is swept sideways with the force of the wind. Towards the end of one violent storm, as calm was gradually restored, I saw the dark grey sky slashed with a vivid rainbow and white birds in an untidy flock were scattered on the wind like ticker-tape.

Though there is beauty in this extreme weather there is also destruction. Most years there is considerable damage to trees, particularly the shallow-rooted walnuts which are often blown over by high winds. Even if they are flattened and are attached by just a root or two, they may survive and carry on producing. Roof tiles skim across the roads like Frisbies, creating a crunchy surface to negotiate, and roads are often washed away by these frequent storms. Vaison la Romaine, in Provence, suffered catastrophic storms a few years ago, when its ancient bridge, together with houses, caravans and people, were washed away. This same storm caused a section of the road to collapse between Beaulieu and our village, and a car was swept into the river, fortunately without injuring anyone. In 2001, there was so much rain that sections of the soft earth embankments beside many roads slid down. The earth is either fine alluvial silt, which is wonderful to cultivate but can be unstable, or solid rock. In fact, much of this limestone rock is not solid at all but as holey as a Gruyère cheese, which accounts for the area being riddled with all those spectacular cave systems,

I have only let the house once in winter, when a young man wanted a quiet place to get away from everybody for Christmas. I just hope he was warm enough. The chill of winter quickly seeps into the stones. There is a strange warm patch in February, which occurs most years, when, Anne tells me, she has enjoyed drinks before lunch on her balcony, wearing a cotton shirt and no jumper. My first visit of the year is around Easter. Some years it is pleasantly warm but unless I have asked the plumber to check the radiators and boiler and to

135

leave the heating on for a week before my arrival it can be freezing as a tomb. I have sat at supper time, wearing thick socks, several jumpers and a scarf, with the heating turned up full blast, a fan heater blasting out 3K at my feet, the door of the boiler room ajar and the oven open, and I still felt cold. Huddling near the log fire upstairs is the only way to thaw out. We can burn logs at least a yard long in the hearth and though they take some effort to haul up the outside steps, the joy of crashing out after a strenuous day in the garden, with a glass of Armagnac and an old movie, in front of a great fire in the enormous fireplace, is worth every bit of hard work.

The stone walls of the kitchen keep the temperature low all year round, for which we are eternally grateful on steamy summer days. Our thermometer by the front door often registers nearly 100°F and the car gauge has shown over 130°F when we've left it in the sun. Thank goodness for air-conditioning in the car. The matting-covered pergola in the front garden is a welcome respite from the midday sun when we want to lunch outside. When we used to cycle to a favourite bathing place by the Dordogne it was a struggle to get up the hills on the way there, but on the return it was always worse. Having pushed the bikes across a bumpy field, up a stony track and then mounted them to fly freewheeling down the hill, the momentum ran out before the bridge, which is followed by an exhausting long upward slope into the village. By the time we got back to the house we were all so sweaty we needed another swim. Of course we love the sunshine, and there is variety. It's not so unremittingly scorching, nor so eye-peelingly brilliant that everyone longs for rain. Summers at Folie seem as hot and long as those I remember from my childhood and student days, when I recall punting and swimming in the River Cam in May. It had to be May, as the university had gone down by the end of the first week of June, and we've got the photos to prove it.

Sometimes we wake to a world of whiteness, when our valley is completely filled with fog, that usually clears by mid-morning. Driving up through it you emerge on the hilltops to a different land of clear sunshine, while the plains and valleys are covered with fog so still that it could be a lake you can see below. Other days there are streaks of thick mist hanging on the folds of the hills, drifting upwards like smoke. One day the girls and I were going to take a trip on the train, which winds in and out of tunnels along the wooded and otherwise inaccessible gorge of the Cère from Biars to Aurillac, in the Auvergne, but it was cancelled due to a fire on the line. We compensated for our disappointment by driving around some lovely countryside we hadn't been to before. The fog clung heavy and thick in the valleys. I was driving very cautiously. Firstly we encountered a narrow suspension bridge, barely wide enough for one car, which loomed eerily out of the mist. It was impossible to see if something was coming towards me. I cautiously advanced. At either end were clustered several armoured cars and lorries. The French army was on manoeuvres. How they had managed to get their vehicles over this tiny bridge is a mystery. Maybe they hadn't. Perhaps they'd approached it from both ends and had not actually crossed over it.

Continuing through the all-consuming mist, we arrived at Turenne, an ancient but tiny castle-crowned hill town, formerly owned by the eponymous Vicomte de Turenne, Marshal-General, friend and favourite of King Louis XIV. He owned everything he could see from his tower as well as much more land beyond. Seeing the town now, no bigger than a small village, one is bewildered at the incredible power these 17th century landowners were able to exercise over their minions. Climbing up through the steep and narrow streets, still shrouded in their enveloping cloak of dense fog, we emerged just below the castle walls into bright sunshine. The castle tower seemed spotlit in the morning rays, which soon broke through the thick layers of mist to give us yet another glorious hot blue-skied day.

Evening sun can light up the woods across the valley with

odd effects, sometimes brilliant gold or smeared with carmine and orange. I have seen a light blue sky streaked with brown, purple and white clouds, with the fierce yellow sun flashing in and out of the layers as it descended, and a random vapour-trail like a careless chalk mark on the blue. Then the bats come out to feed, silently darting across the darkening sky, while owls make coded conversation from tree to tree. On rare and magical nights glow-worms flash their secret messages from the garden wall. Some nights, over the hills opposite, the huge moon rises like a freed balloon. Its climb is so swift, it seems amazing it then takes all night to traverse the sky. Other nights it can barely be glimpsed through drifting clouds which look like a shredded grey shawl. How wonderful and diverse nature is. How lucky we are to see so much beauty, even if it does bite at times.

Chapter 13
'FRIENDS' and 'NEIGHBOURS'

It is often said that you do not really know your friends until you have lived with them. People I invite to share Folie for a week or two, hopefully are more polite and old-fashioned in their outlook than the 'Friends' and 'Neighbours' in the TV shows, and take pains to avoid conflict and confrontation. However, holidays can be tricky if you wrongly assess what your friends will be like when they share your house. The timing of baths and showers, and the commandeering of the bathroom for shaving (men always seem to take so much longer in the bathroom than women, even their showers go on for twice the time) can be a source of uncomfortable disagreement. Mostly, the friends I have asked to accompany me to La Folie Verte have proved themselves true friends, sharing chores and enjoying the house and its environment as much as I do and their idiosyncratic foibles have been easy to accommodate.

There have been the occasional mistakes, however. Some of the minor failures have proved a source of humour later, though at the time others required a great deal of patience and silent counting before an apparently cheerful face could be put on again. A friend of Glyn, a painter friend, found it quite impossible to remember to put down the loo seat. Glyn drew me a cartoon of an open loo, a man walking away, hands protecting his manhood and a God-like hand (meant to be mine) pointing from a great cloud. The caption is in French but translates as, "Madame insists that you put the seat down after use." I still get the odd guest who irritatingly fails to comply! I am, I admit, ridiculously obsessive (and possibly snobbish) about some of my quirks. I cannot understand why other people do not realise that the poppies decorating the dinner and tea plates should grow from the bottom. It seems so logical to me, and the table looks so much nicer when the plates are placed symmetrically.

Sometimes Glyn offered to do the washing up. At first I thought this very generous, though I do not wield a drying-up cloth very effectively and am a quick washer-up. However, very soon I regretted taking up his kind suggestion as I stood, bravely controlling my increasing frustration at the slow production of things to dry. Glyn's method is to take one plate, knife, glass or whatever at a time, wash it with a brush in the sudsy water then turn on the tap over the second sink and rinse each item carefully under the running water before placing it on the draining board. I was swift to take over his duties at the sink.

Another annoyance I need to air concerns people who ask to visit Sarlat for the Saturday morning market and then fail to get up early enough to get there. Having been advised that the journey takes an hour and 20 minutes, it was maddening to find one lady still in her dressing-gown at the appointed hour, and even more so when I heard her rudely mutter, "Rush, rush,

rush," under her breath as I chivvied her to get ready. She was not invited again.

Drinking habits (and I don't mean alcoholics) sometimes cause minor difficulties. Jenny (of the snails) will only drink tea from a china cup, never a pottery mug. As the only bone china items to be found at Folie are the rather small coffee cans we use after dinner, she had to keep on pouring cup after cup to be satisfied. A French visitor requested a tisane of lemon balm. On this occasion it was Jenny who unwittingly came to the rescue. Some years before, she had planted some of this herb under my magnolia tree, and it produced just enough leaves to make the tea Maïte required during her three-day visit. Her husband, Robert, brought remarkably generous compensation for this little request in the form of a dozen wine glasses and three magnums of excellent wine from his own vineyard. They can come again!

Most of my memories of a holiday at Easter one year, with Linda, a lady I hadn't known very well before asking her, are centred on Sarlat and Rocamadour. Linda went on a spending spree of stupendous proportions. Being Easter, the chocolate shops were filled with the most enticing array of gorgeously decorated eggs, rabbits and chickens. Tiny shiny eggs were heaped in china dishes or eggcups, tied up with crackly cellophane paper and ribbons and embellished with little artificial flowers or fluffy miniature chicks. Linda was enchanted, so much of our morning at Sarlat was spent selecting the prettiest arrangements, at least one for every member of her family. Then she discovered a tasteful Interiors shop, where she chose table linen, baskets and napkin rings. Actually, I succumbed and bought some napkin rings as well. They are beautifully carved of wood and cleverly painted to look like apples and pears, green, yellow or red, so making it easy to distinguish whose is whose when laying the table. Eventually, I had to leave Linda, surrounded by overflowing bags and packages, while I retrieved the car, as even between us there was too much to carry. She repeated the exercise at Rocamadour. It was all enormous fun, helping an even more enthusiastic shopper than myself to spend money.

My least favourite visitors are those who think we are at Folie for a holiday! Well of course we are but the basic duties like washing up, keeping the bathroom clean and tidy, and the living room respectable have to be done in spite of the desire to relax. Fortunately I haven't entertained too many of the lazy type. My most favourite friends are those who positively enjoy taking on the challenge of helping in a practical way to make the house even more comfortable than it is already. These paragons of virtue put up shelves, repair bikes and canoes, help prune shrubs and delight in pyromania (having huge and noisy bonfires when we're permitted by law, in the spring and autumn). The bamboo, which leers and looms over the end of our garden, needs to be hacked back regularly from its insidious encroachment. Its tough roots radiate around a central spear which tunnels sideways from the parent plant and then emerges abruptly in the middle of a flowerbed, growing a metre or more a year. When burnt, the stems explode with bangs like gunshot and the leaves crackle loudly as they shrivel, causing the neighbours to come inquisitively up the track to see what is going on. Our dear friends Jack and Helen, who have enjoyed the house with their family and joined us for several holidays in the summer, fall into this energetic category. Jack is undoubtedly hyperactive. On returning from a day out, and after the briefest gulp of tea, he is ready, indeed eager, to tackle some new project. I have to think up several essential jobs each year to keep him busy.

Geraldine is a keen and talented photographer. Her husband will rarely pause long enough for her to capture a castle, let alone a fleeting image, a dramatic sky or a bird. I obviously pleased her enormously, not only by stopping to allow her to get out of the car to take photos, but also telling her when I knew there was a good subject down the road so she could prepare her camera in advance. It was she who was the trigger for a new friendship, arrived at quite accidentally. We had been touring an area a few miles away and stopped in a pretty, well-known village, famous for its row of partly ruined chateaux along a narrow ridge. I sat at the bar, painting a small water-colour, while she wandered around the quaint old lanes. A middle-aged man in casual working clothes had walked across the road to look briefly at what I was doing, and commented on it with a few words of encouragement, and then wandered off to do some gardening, pushing a wheelbarrow near some old iron gates. On Geraldine's return I packed up my things and we walked to my car, parked near these high metal gates.

"What does that mean," asked Geraldine, indicating a sign on the wall.

"It's a slightly strange way of saying 'Private, No Entry'," I replied, at which the man, now with his wife, said, "Would you like to go in?"

We nodded eagerly, realising that we were standing by the entrance to the largest of the chateaux.

"Do you own it?" I queried.

"Yes," he said, "but we don't live in it. We live in a house in the grounds."

Welcoming us into the garden the couple invited us to climb the newly constructed concrete stairs to the top of the main tower to take photos. Later, the owners told us that they had restored the roof of the tower to preserve the buildings for the future, not to live in, and that, in fact, they spent at least half of the year in Paris where Madame was an English teacher. We exchanged names and addresses, sent copies of the photos we had taken and kept in touch.

A year or so later, they suggested I took part in a painting competition held annually in their village. Artists, amateur or professional, turn up at about 8am to register and have their paper or canvas stamped with the village insignia and the date, to avoid cheating (otherwise competitors could bring along paintings they had worked on for days). A simple lunch is available, but many painters don't take a break as they need all the time to finish before the 3 o'clock deadline for watercolours

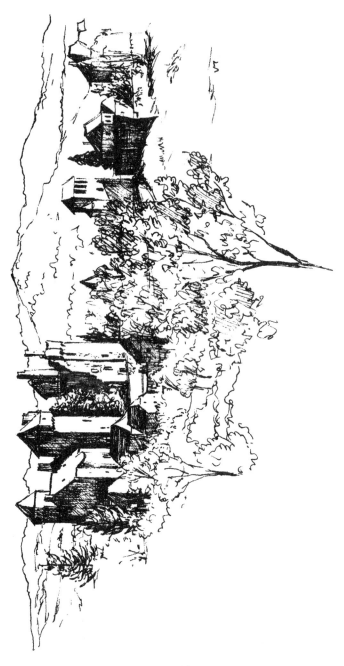

Evening sun at Curemonte

or the 4pm time for oils. Everyone taking part selects a view they like best and sets to work in any medium they choose. The most obvious spots are occupied quickly as the artists set out their paints, erect easels and install themselves comfortably (or not) on chairs and stools they have brought. I began to sketch out the elementary placing of a fine Renaissance house and the surrounding buildings, with a view down a grassy path into the countryside; a nice composition. But I was sitting in a rather populous lane where passers-by wanted to stand and chat. After 1½ hours, I decided it wasn't working at all. The proportions of the tower I had chosen were wrong. I had rubbed it out, started again and still didn't like it. Gathering up my equipment and stool, I decided to explore the back lanes again. I began another drawing in a quiet corner, where few wandering tourists paused to look over my shoulder, or distract me with inane conversation.

The paper I had chosen was a greyish Italian handmade paper, speckled with flecks of different colours, appropriate for depicting the textures of crumbling stone, but it had a problem. I had a problem! After I had drawn the semi-derelict building, with leaning chimneys and falling in windows, and its junk-filled lean-to, I mixed some blue paint for the sky, applied a streak of it and attempted to spread the paint as a wash. The paper absorbed the paint instantly, like blotting paper. It had not been finished with size, as I had expected it to be. Some areas of the picture ended up with at least 5 or 6 layers of paint in order to get the depth of colour I needed - not what one is meant to do with a watercolour. I spent the lunch hour with Henri, my kind gardener (and Lord of the Manor) keeping an eye on my wellbeing, constantly filling my glass with red wine, saying it would help me to work better. With about an hour to go to the official handing-in time I returned to work. I added a thin black ink line to my watercolour to give it definition and further texture and submitted it. I even had enough spare time after my much delayed start, to do another pencil and wash drawing. The residents of Curemonte generously awarded me the prize for the painting, which they considered most represented their village. It was at the prize-giving ceremony that I discovered that my friends from the chateau were the organisers (though not the judges) of the competition.

Two other houses in our village are owned by English people. One, sadly underused since the couple's divorce, was built to their design as they couldn't find a suitable house to buy. This amazes me, as the estate agent's windows are full of a range of property at prices from the ridiculously cheap, being advertised as a 'house for the DIY enthusiast', to fully finished and highly desirable homes at rather higher prices. The other house, an old one like mine but nearer the river, has changed hands once since we bought Folie. The new owners are a sweet and generous couple, a few years older than me, who talk enthusiastically about the possibilities their house has for improvement. But they never quite get round to doing anything. It's all too easy to fall into the 'laissez-faire' attitude of the French, who regard the maintenance of the exteriors of their houses as an unnecessary luxury. All these kind neighbours have become friends. Though our holiday dates rarely overlap, when they do, we make a point of getting together for a meal or drinks. None of us wishes to live in each other's pockets, but it is pleasant to share experiences and to have the occasional relaxed conversation in English. These friends need to be nurtured.

There would be no point in having a house in a village if you intend to ignore or fail to relate to your neighbours in a courteous way, accepting the differences in manners and culture. You might as well be in the wilds of nowhere if you don't attempt to be friendly. But that does rely on at least a smattering of French. We all try very hard with our French, but will never learn to prattle with colloquial fluency. Conversations are sometimes a bit one-sided, and although I often get parts of verbs wrong, no one seems to mind. Generally I get the gist of what is being said. It is when I am included in a three or four-way conversation, and the villagers are not making any special effort to simplify their language (and why should they, just to make it easier for me), that I get lost in the complexities of French grammar. One ends up smiling and nodding in a wise and solemn way, often having only the vaguest notion of what they're talking about. I would definitely rather have the comfort of knowing that there is always someone down the lane to help in an emergency, than have exclusive privacy in a cottage in a field with no neighbours.

It seems as if the area attracts a certain type of person, one who does not require a great deal in the way of entertainment or sophistication. We all enjoy the country life. Other friends, who've taken advantage of people's desire to experience this life, include an English couple who converted most of a nearby mediæval chateau into a B&B. Jill, who appears deceptively frail, with her thin, blond good-looks, was frequently left to cope on her own while Joe was in England running other businesses. She undertook the raising of pigs, chickens and geese, even doing her own butchering on occasion. She cooked wonderful meals, made the soft furnishings, painted bedrooms and attended to guests, all with a relaxed grace and a strength belied by her fragile physique. Unfortunately, following a break-up, she is no longer at the chateau. I had often hankered after running a music course there, as they had a fine grand piano in the great salon which would have made a perfect rehearsal room. There is much good music performed in the area during the summer, at the various churches and at the Abbatiale in Beaulieu, so a concert at the end of a high standard choral course would have been much appreciated.

My cleaner, Martine, and her two daughters, offer me four mwa-mwa air-kisses when we meet, and I exchange handshakes with Pierre, her husband, garden-rubbish clearer, odd-job man and grass cutter. Each year I send them proper Christmas presents, but have also given Pierre my old motorbike and several tatty push-bikes. Pierre, like Jack, is a DIY enthusiast, though mechanical things and computers please him best. He cannibalises junk to make more useful machines, such as his scary strimmer, which has a circular saw blade for a cutting-head, perfect for attacking my rampant bamboo. I hope to heaven his engineering is sound, as I hate to think of the damage he could do himself if the blade ever worked itself loose. I am sure that our relationship is seen with suspicion by those who see themselves as superior... land-owning farmers. Some of these have declined my drinks invitations when they knew some folk of more humble status were also invited. In the village several of my neighbours are friendly, but it is difficult to break the barriers between courtesies and true friendships. Although I have invited a few of my neighbours in for a drink, including the Mayor and his wife, I'd be surprised to get a return invitation. We will be forever outsiders. Even Anne, who speaks excellent French and has lived in her village for about 20 years, is still not automatically invited to village functions or to people's homes. Perhaps a Frenchman's home is more his castle than an Englishman's.

Chapter 14

PROBLEM PAGE

I sometimes wonder why I bother with letting the house, though I know the answer. If I didn't, I wouldn't have it at all. Tony made the proviso that the house 'washed its own face'; that income from lettings would pay for the basic running expenses, cleaning, grass cutting, gas cylinders, local taxes, water consumption, oil for the boiler, telephone and electricity. It was never the intention to buy a house as an investment, and it is only in the last two years, when prices have suddenly jumped, that the cost of Folie, and the improvements we have made would raise an equal sum if we chose to sell up. Any profits have been ploughed back so far, and the bank still owns a proportion of it. On the whole, letting has been relatively trouble-free and not too time-consuming. I manage the paper work, putting eye-catching postcards into post office and paper shop windows, on notice boards at Tony's office and at the choir I sing with in London. Some replies come from unexpected sources, as visitors to Surrey from distant parts of Britain see the adverts. A few guests have returned several years running, or have passed on the information to their friends if they have had a good time. Comments about improvements in the Vistors' Book are noted and acted upon where possible, money permitting. A suggestion for the loo and basin in the loft took a few years of saving to afford. A toaster was a little easier to supply.

However, some people come with unreasonably high expectations. I try to gauge whether potential guests are suitable for the house. Those who are looking for a Mediterranean villa, with en-suite bathrooms, white tiled floors everywhere and a daily maid will be disappointed, as just a few people have been. Others cannot tolerate the idea of spiders or dust. I attempt to describe the house accurately in my publicity, and always honestly answer any questions when phoned for information. There's no point in not telling the truth about the house, as guests will only be unhappy if they arrive to find it different from how they envisaged it. Usually I am right about people I have only heard once on the phone. Some, I have to say, I have lied to, saying the house is booked, because I don't like the sound of them or their attitude. After all, it is my home and I am not obliged to let to people I don't fancy. The people who are enthusiastic, looking forward to discovering a new area, who ask what the children might do and are not put off by suggestions of swimming in the river or lakes, or going to caves, or those who enjoy walking or cycling, are people I want to let to. I do, however, sometimes get it wrong.

Briefly, I shall mention a few of the more bizarre and unpleasant things my guests have done over the years. Beds have been jumped on, pushing the springy slats onto the floor. They are very difficult to slot back into place. My beer has been drunk by teenagers, who left several bottles under the beds as evidence of their rebelliousness. A number of empties were also slung out of the window into the garden. A radio and garden chairs have been broken and the damage denied. Pillows have had to be burnt after children have been sick on them. My sheets have been borrowed and returned, dirty, to my chest of drawers. Bedcovers are frequently left screwed up in cupboards. The list could continue but these are just some of the problems of letting a holiday house.

The trouble with anything that is left in the wrong place is that the next people to come have no idea of how things ought to look. One of the daftest, and potentially the most dangerous thing I often find, is that plugs are taken out and changed around. The circuit cannot take too many powerful electrical items being used at once, and certainly not two in one socket. One year I even found the television all covered with soot and rain as it had been moved and left in the fireplace.

My list of instructions to incoming guests gets longer and longer each year as people do more and more stupid things. I always forgive those who own up to their accidents, though it was a little difficult to smile graciously as I was told of one lady who managed to drop four irreplaceable plates in one go. The china I originally chose went rapidly out of production, so every time I see matching plates or teapots at charity shops or boot fairs I buy it. I think I have three teapots and one spare lid put away now! Neither was I very pleased to hear that the marble we had saved from the old dresser, which was used as a table top in the garden, had been knocked off its base and smashed, but the culprits did phone and apologise. I was also taken aback to hear that someone had managed to drop and break a large and very heayy Le Creuset casserole dish on my newly tiled floor. They promised to send money for a replacement, but it never came, even after two reminders. Amazingly the tiles had survived even if the cast-iron pot had not. The glass topped coffee table in the living room is, as yet, unbroken... after 13 years, with small children on the loose. Its time must be up soon.

In the store cupboards in the kitchen I leave lots of basic

stores – enough to make a simple meal on the first night, if necessary. Visitors are asked to 'replace anything that they finish or is very nearly finished, and to have consideration for those following them'. Often I have arrived to find two teaspoons of coffee, a few sheets of loo paper, and several broken light bulbs. Inconsiderate folk have, on occasion, left the waste bins full and the fridge not wedged open, encouraging a livid growth of nasty multicoloured moulds. I find puzzle pieces scattered regularly on the floor or among the bowls of *pot pourri*. And don't even think of having a game of cards, unless you have brought your own packs. None of mine will be complete. I can't begin to count the belongings left behind in the boiler room: socks, towels, drying-up cloths, shorts and various unmentionables. Last summer I commented on the fact that there only seemed to be nine folding chairs in the kitchen, rather than ten. I searched for the missing chair but assumed that it had been broken and thrown away without the perpetrator telling me. In October I decided to turn all the mattresses, as they had not been done that year. Under the mattress in the main bedroom was the chair, unbroken. Presumably someone had found the bed too soft and had placed the chair there to create a firmer base. An odd thing to do, since when folded those chairs are not exactly flat. I suppose they had just forgotten about it when they left. I wonder how many of the guests that summer had slept on it, without knowing, thinking that I had provided a miserably lumpy bed.

Sometimes we have caused our own problems, like blocking the loo when an 'all girlie' group has been staying at the house. Monsieur Farge was called immediately when this happened one morning, but took all day to find the time to come. Meanwhile, the public village facilities were occupied rather more than usual. Sometimes, however, the problems are not of our making, such as the Easter I arrived to find two inches of water swilling around the kitchen and lobby. Actually, it was even deeper towards the back of the house, as the floor was not level. My entire luggage was abandoned in the car while I found out where the water was leaking from. A tiny hole in the pipe, by the outside tap, was spraying a fine mist through a vent leading to the storage cupboards and thence the floor. The plumber was unable to come until the following day, so I rigged up a piece of plastic to stop the water coming in and to divert it away from the wall and down the garden. Then I swept and mopped the floor, using all my spare towels, until most of the water was outside rather than in. After this I had to remove and wipe dry soaked stores, or throw away the things that had been totally ruined from the sodden cupboards. What could be rescued had to be stored elsewhere, to dry out. A lovely old striped Greek rug literally dropped into shreds as I picked it up. It was about eight in the evening before I could start emptying the car, making my bed, and putting together a simple supper. I was exhausted, having to face a flood on my own after a seven-hour drive, and it made me question the sanity of having a holiday house abroad. As the damp walls dried out, stains were left and some of the paint flaked off, in places a foot or more up the wall, where the water had penetrated the plaster. The concrete kitchen floor, which was then covered with old thermoplastic tiles, took a long time to dry out, and as it did the tiles lifted and cracked. The carpenter came at the end of my stay to replace the store cupboard shelves, though the residual damp in the walls meant that even the replacements have warped. When he removed the old chipboard shelves the water ran in streams out of the ends of the boards. The light at the end of this awful tunnel was a lovely new tiled floor, paid for by the insurance company.

If I am asked whether I have ever regretted buying a house in France, my response is an emphatic "No". It was bought for fun. Anyone taking on a project as big as mine, let alone buying something even more rundown, who thinks they will make money out of it, is almost sure to be disappointed and out of pocket. Although French property prices have risen considerably in the last few years it must be borne in mind that capital gains tax is high. A resale after only a few years will result in a loss, even though improvements can be offset against the increased price. One is advised to keep every bill for work or materials in case there is a need to sell up. Capital gains tax reduces a little each year, eventually to nothing, but this system is designed to discourage speculative purchasers trying to make a quick profit. The only good reason for buying a foreign property is to use it regularly for holidays.

As I clean, wash and iron linens, paint walls, tidy the garden and sort everything back into its proper place, I sometimes think I spend more time getting the house in order for my paying guests than enjoying it myself. But I also know that it gives me a great deal of pleasure to make the house neat and welcoming. It is 'home'. Even Jack and Helen say it's home to them. The fact that it is the same, when I return, or maybe subtly improved (by the addition of a washing machine or a new cooker) makes La Folie Verte into the relaxing holiday house everyone enjoys. My original intention was to have a place to paint, with my own belongings around me and to create a comfortable environment, which I believe I have done. Now I find pruning the shrubs and potting the geraniums in the Spring equally rewarding. I still paint a little, but it is a less important factor in my life than it was. I am more enthusiastic to get out and about to see yet more intriguing natural or historical sites than to record a limited number in paint and never get to see the rest. So even if I spend time preparing the house for others to use, my own time there is mostly very pleasurable. The rewards far outweigh the problems.

VT

Sundae

Chapter 15

ENGLAND v FRANCE

Life in the Corrèze never moves at the pace of a football match. Everything is extremely stately, except for some summer tourist traffic. A trip to the shops for a couple of days' supplies often takes most of the morning. Shops are usually open from 9am until 12 noon, and then again from 3pm to 6 or 7pm. Even some of the large stores selling furniture or kitchen equipment close for a lunch hour, or three. You have to time a shopping trip carefully. I have heard of people having loaded up a trolley with goods arriving at the checkout, only to find that the shop is closing, and they have to return after lunch to pay and collect their shopping. Once, with Pippa, we didn't realise that the clocks had changed in the autumn and couldn't understand why the shops were closing. For two days we lived in another time to everyone else. It was only when Anne arrived an hour early, or so we thought, for dinner, that we dis-covered our mistake. She roared with laughter and was quite happy to sit with a glass of kir while we buzzed around getting the meal together.

When I make an excursion to Brive, I take in the antiques shop and the DIY shop on my way to the hypermarket, where I arrive in time for lunch. The food is first-rate, probably sub-sidised. You can eat salmon and rice with a delicious sauce for about £3. Wine comes out of a help-yourself barrel, red or rosé, and works out at 50p for two glasses. There are microwave ovens to use for free if your main course has got cold while you are eating your salad or starter. A token is sold at the cash desk for a hot help-yourself coffee from machines strategically placed at several points around the restaurant. No queuing up for a second time, after your meal is finished, or a cooling cof-fee under an upturned saucer here. When the girls and I first went there, about 13 years ago, you could serve yourself with chocolate mousse from a large bowl. It was superb, just like home-made, and we all greedily heaped our tall sundae dish-es as high as possible. Sadly it now comes in more modest pre-served portions, but still tastes just as good.

After this feast I wander around the aisles at a less hectic pace than I would have done without the preceding lunch. Certain items are massively cheaper than home. Goodies like canned *confit* of duck are only available in the very best deli-catessens in England but can be found at any hypermarket. Pippa introduced me to a delicious lemon or grapefruit squash called Pulco, which has a lot less sugar in it than our usual vari-eties. We are totally hooked on iced tea *(Thé à la Pêche)* made by Liptons. As a refreshing summer drink it is hard to beat. English supermarkets are now stocking it, but in tiny cans rather than enormous bottles and at more than three times the price. Ground almonds and pure essences of both almonds and vanilla, jars of *pâté* or *cassoulet* and, of course wine, in quantity, are good value. Packets of easy to cook bread mix, chocolate mousse, and frangipane flan filling all find their way into my shopping, so my trolley is always well heaped by the checkout. By the time I have finished here, the garden centre and the clothes, shoe, fabric and specialist shops in town will have re-opened for me to browse, indulging in very satisfactory retail therapy at leisure.

Locally, in Beaulieu, the shops open on Sunday mornings and close all day on Monday. Twice a month, on Fridays, there is a market, when everyone is out and about. People come from miles around, as much to meet friends – greeting neighbours with the traditional handshake and close friends with as many as four cheek-kisses, or to have a drink or a coffee – as to shop for groceries. You are encouraged, particularly at market stalls, to choose your own fruit and vegetables and people deliberate for ages over the best tomatoes, apricots or whatever, putting their carefully selected goods into little plastic mesh baskets for weighing. Every item is picked up, examined, approved or rejected. Beans can be chosen individually, if you like. You are never palmed off with under or over-ripe fruit, or vegetables of a different standard to those on display as sometimes happens in markets in England. It is striking that fresh food is sold uncovered and exposed to the sun – fish, oysters, bread, vats of olives, hams and *saucisses*. Trading standards officers would be down on this casual display like a ton of bricks at home. The food seems to come to no harm with this careless attitude to hygiene. We haven't suffered either with the tummy bugs you might expect – I am sure we are all far too obsessed with clean-liness. As for weights and measures, traders often use rusty old hand-held balances (frequently seen at junk markets) on which they hang a plastic bag full of your selected vegetables. You are usually likely to get more for your money this way, as these scales are only accurate if time is taken to wait until the bag stops swinging and the bar is level. No one bothers if you get more or less. One may ask for *'une livre,'* 'a pound,' of produce. This is actually half a kilo, and weighs a little more than an English pound, but it is a useful measure for those of us who haven't gone metric yet.

Cheeses can be tasted before a decision is made. A sliver will be cut off and passed over the van's high counter. Discussion among the waiting buyers about the differences between farmhouse, mild or mature Cantal cheese takes several minutes. It is most important to everyone that you buy what pleases you. At the butcher's your chosen cut of meat will be meticulously prepared, all extraneous fat cut off, except that which has been deliberately and neatly tied on, to self-baste your joint. Then the best recipe or precise time for cooking the piece of meat will be suggested. And no one seems to mind waiting. Old-world courtesies still survive and a willingness to serve graciously seems almost universal. Even in the bigger supermarkets you are greeted at the delicatessen counter with a ready *"Bonjour"*. On parting you are wished a sincere farewell. It never sounds as casual as "Have a good day" in England or America. Admittedly some shops in England are getting the message that the shopper, the one with the dosh, deserves to be treated better. Nothing is more irritating than waiting for an assistant to finish her conversation with a friend before attending to your needs. This truly rarely happens in the more rural parts of France.

Many French shops have a charming old-fashioned feel to them, in all but the most touristy towns. Display is merely to show what is in stock. Goods are often left in the windows for weeks on end, gently fading in the sun. DIY and hardware stores heap up their wares in apparently random order, or pile more or less similar things into baskets. The layout is quite chaotic and to find anything, you have to walk around apparenty abandoned brooms or washing machines and ironing boards, all seemingly carefully placed to create a veritable maze. It is for this delightful retro-style of living that we English descend on south-west France in such hoards in the summer months.

At times, though, however rarely, I wish that the two countries were more similar. I had enormous difficulty finding a telephone cable to connect to my laptop computer. I was informed that a shop selling such items was to be found in Toulouse, two and a half hours drive away. Not even Brive, a major industrial town 25 miles north of us, could offer a suitable computer shop. When we are used to seeing such emporia on every street corner, it made France appear very backward. However, Pierre managed to find me one from somewhere. I didn't ask where; I was just grateful. Then I found that didn't work either and I needed a small decoder, costing another £20, to enable the French telephone system to talk to the English one.

Anne remarks that she can live, quite contentedly, on a lot less than we think we need in England. What costs much more in France is Social Security, but since their hospitals can offer a hip replacement in just four weeks from a first appointment, perhaps it's worth the extra cash. In your 70s, if you live that long, you don't have to pay any more local rates, which is a great help for impoverished pensioners. For everyday living you need less money, partly because social occasions are fewer and no one minds what you wear. Fashion may be seen in magazines, but not on the general population. The workman still wears his 'blues' (bright blue dungarees or boiler suits) and a flat cap most days. His wife will have bought her all-enveloping, flower-print pinny from a market stall and will put it on every day, over her plain jumper and woollen skirt, to do her chores. Everyone helps out in the fields, even really old people still cut and gather hay by hand for the animals they keep in barns and sheds near their homes. Even in quite smart restaurants diners do not dress up and the men rarely put on a jacket. The most likely place to see the men dressed in tweed, denim or corduroy jackets and black berets, is at a 'Concourse des Animaux', when they bring their finest beasts to be judged in the town square. Beaulieu hosts these smelly, messy competitions regularly, indeed not so long ago a regular cattle market was held under the trees in one of the *'Places'*. One is reluctant these days to categorise anyone, but the wrinkled, weather-beaten and immensely dignified faces of the farmers spell 'peasant'. Their life is a hard one, working to make a sparse living on a few acres. French inheritance law creates a lot of problems, as land and property has to be divided among surviving members of the family. Many farms have been split up so many times that they are now barely big enough to support a family, and unless one brother can buy out another, both suffer the effects of an outdated system. It may be logically fair, but actually causes hardship and distress.

Another reason for needing less money is that interior design is confined to incomers and social climbers. The French are not as passionate about 'keeping up with the Joneses' as the English suburban house owner. What the residents think of our desire to buy and restore what they regard as old-fashioned, tumbledown hovels I can only surmise. Their taste is generally for new houses in garish modern taste, often embellished, as the old ones were, with hideous glass porches and over-elaborate and inappropriate wrought iron work. These little boxes usually perch on a mound of cropped grass, underneath which is a practical cellar. Neat shrubs line the drive and pots of geraniums decorate the terrace edges. Everything is very tidy and precise, but soulless, while we foreigners want the old stone cottages and farmhouses for their old-world charm. We prefer the walls to be uneven. We don't mind if the floors are not level or if the house is not on main drainage. The uneven rooflines give us pleasure, as do the overgrown gardens we love to tame. There is no doubt that the average English-owned cottage has a prettier garden than those which grace most French-owned houses, even allowing for long absences during which weeds grow rapaciously. The French 'do' pots in a big way, but their gardens often feel sterile. It is no wonder that so many old houses are on the market. Our own was for sale for three years before we arrived. The French do not want to be bothered with these semi-derelict buildings. Rural residents appear content to live in simple style, leaving great cracks in exterior walls unfilled and paint faded and peeling. As long as the house doesn't seem to be falling down they'll leave it to grow old gracefully (unlike the old ladies' hair, which is rarely grey, more often vivid red, tightly permed or brutally shorn).

The class system in France is at least as active as in England. 'Trade' may not be looked down upon quite as much as it used to be but there is a definite hierarchy. Those on the parish council and of course the mayor (and there is one of those in every village or group of hamlets), are at the top of the ladder, together with the biggest landowner, who may be one of the former as well. Where we holiday home owners come in the hierarchy I am not sure. Maybe, hopefully, we are not counted – just regarded as oddities, probably envied for our spare cash and as apparently wealthy folk there to be fleeced sometimes. As a 'non-belonger' it is best to smile and pay up if you want to keep everyone sweet. It is also as well to follow the local laws, if you can find out what they are. I have been warned not to have bonfires during the forbidden months in summer, even after heavy rain, as I may be 'shopped' by those less favourable to my presence in the village. In some areas such as Brittany, there has been a movement against the British, whom the local people think have taken over their homeland. Fortunately we have not encountered this uncomfortable resentment in the Corrèze. We may never be accepted completely, but the longer we're albeit temporary residents the more we are tolerated, as long as we follow the social rules.

A captivating custom that has survived into the 21st century is the different way weddings are conducted. In the villages you often pass houses where the drive has been decorated with little fir trees, with what look like pink and white paper handkerchiefs tied onto their branches. This strange custom signifies the house of a bride, though the trees are left for weeks after the wedding, sometimes until they are sad and brown. Guests going to or from a wedding in convoy toot their carhorns loudly and proclaim their destination with scraps of pink and white net tied to their car aerials. The ladies of the village collect heaps of branches from evergreen trees to make a path to the porch and to decorate the arch over the door of the church. Flowers are cut from their own gardens to tie onto the branches and to fill the church vases. In fact, the marriage will already have taken place in the Mairie, either that day or the previous one, so the Catholic Church service is more of a Blessing with Communion. I attended one of these seemingly interminable services and found it amusing to note the differences in the congregations. In England, one is expected to talk in hushed voices before the bride arrives, and to make as little fuss as possible about where to sit, who the other guests are and what they are wearing. In France, it is a great time for loud conversations across the pews. Everyone wants to greet old friends and relations (four kisses each at least), and the general chatter continues unabated throughout the ceremony. Children get up and wander about, people go outside for a smoke, uninvited visitors crane their heads from the doors for a better view and no one objects to any of it. As long as everyone is having a good time.

A less attractive habit of the French is to build vast factories, warehouses and out-of-town shops on greenfield sites. Many of these sell building materials. Monsieur Bricolage is everywhere. There are wood yards and stone yards, roofing tiles, car showrooms, garages for specialised car repairs, *dépôts de vente* (bring and buy, sale or return, junk shops), furniture and fabric stores and swimming pool installers. These unsightly sheds sometimes cluster together in groups, or stand exposed and isolated next to main roads in the most unlikely places. Andros have been allowed to build a shiny metal-walled factory as big as an aircraft hangar just outside Beaulieu. In order to widen the road for turning lorries, a fine row of roadside trees was cut down, making the huge structure even more visible. Service roads, recently constructed, indicate that this development will not be the last, but I feel that large stores and small factories could generally be sited in less obtrusive locations. I am not against out-of-town shopping centres. In France, hypermarkets do not appear to affect the independent town centre shops too disastrously, most of which appear to be thriving. You do not see very many shops remaining empty for long, and there is certainly not as much temporary occupation of premises by fly-by-night traders selling cheap tat as in Britain. The French rarely ruin their city centres with inappropriate, hideous modern glass and concrete buildings, as has been encouraged by heathen council officers in many English historic towns. The charm of old shops is respected and their stylish old-fashioned wooden surrounds, painted in faded *fin de siècle* lettering, are a delight to the eye. Strange, then, that the French choose to live in modern houses.

An avenue of fine beech trees has been cut down and grubbed out on the road to Tulle, not for road widening, but because too many people are crashing into them. Standards of driving are very variable. In wet weather the speed limit goes down by 10 miles an hour; however, travelling on the Paris - Le Havre motorway on a wet Friday evening I'm inclined to doubt that the French take this rule to heart. I have been overtaken by cars going at least 100mph. I know, because I am driving too fast as well, hurrying for my evening boat. On motorways the lane discipline is mostly much better than in England, even lorries move back into the inside lane after passing, though they drive much faster than the permitted speed limits. Someone wishing to overtake (and they invariably will, especially when they see a car with English plates ahead), will put on his left flasher to indicate his intention to the driver in front and then move back in again after the manoeuvre. But while flashing he is probably tail-gating, terrifyingly.

Rural drivers have not necessarily absorbed the law that *priorité à droite* has been abandoned. Recently a large van swung out of a side road, totally ignoring the fact that I was nearly at the junction on a somewhat bigger road. I blasted my horn and stood on my brakes. Drawing level I wound down my window to remonstrate with him, but his immediate response was *"priorité à droite"* accompanied by a typically Gallic shrug. He didn't wait to hear my plaintive reply that it didn't exist any more. One has to be patient on the narrow and winding local roads when delayed by tractors, ancient beret-clad farmers in their rattle-traps, which would never pass an MOT, and their increasingly rare 2CVs. But when the roads are clear, driving is a pleasure. The surfaces are smooth and rarely are allowed to suffer with English-style, axle-breaking potholes, even on the tiniest lanes. France is a big country, with a relatively small population, especially out of the main conurbations. Some days you can be driving on a motorway with absolutely no other car visible in either direction. After the M25 that is pure bliss, but weird. I've sometimes wondered if I am on a finished motorway at all, or whether I've strayed onto a road under construction and I will shortly come to a grinding halt at a cluster of bulldozers.

Café culture has spread worldwide, but still not to the commonplace extent that it exists in France. The workmen will still visit their local bar at breakfast time for a *café complet*, coffee, a croissant, or half a baguette with jam, followed by a glass of something strong, a brandy, pastis or flavoured *eau de vie*. They stand, chatting in groups, or alone at the 'zinc' (more likely 'Formica' now), while only women, tourists or the very old sit at the cheap plastic-topped tables. At mid-morning the bars are full of customers drinking strong but milky coffee. Lunchtime sees a proliferation of *croque-monsieurs*, or *madames*, with a fried or poached egg on top of the toasted cheese, or a 'sandwich', actually half of a baguette filled with cheese, ham or both. Coffee will now be strong, small and black. Many people will not drink any more coffee, unless it is decaffeinated, after lunch, as there is a great belief in the theory that it prevents sleeping at night. You may see tea with lemon, a *citron-pressé*, (hopefully, correctly made with freshly-squeezed lemon juice, some tubes of sugar and a large jug of water, to top it up), or more likely coke, wine or something stronger, drunk from afternoon onwards. But whatever time it is, the cafés will be full.

The girls used to pretend to be French and liked to sit over a drink, feeling superior to English summer visitors, especially somewhere like Sarlat. So often the English make themselves very conspicuous in their too-short shorts, vests and strappy tee-shirts, dark socks and sandals or dirty trainers which mark them out from the more discreetly, appropriately and soberly dressed French. I wouldn't say that the locals are in any way chic. This isn't Paris or the South of France in terms of sartorial elegance but then neither do the French dress as if they were on a beach. In Beaulieu one traditionally decorated and furnished café is usually populated by the middle-aged and elderly. Inside are spindly metal chairs with hard plastic seats, or narrow benches upholstered in stained fabrics of hard-to-determine colour, while those outside are either stretchy, multicoloured plastic cord, woven around a metal frame, or rigid, hip-crunching ones from a garden centre. Another bar is occupied almost exclusively by the young, who noisily spill out onto the pavement every evening. Noise from a jukebox and the youngsters' animated chatter is tolerated, as long as they go home around midnight. They seem a good-natured, talkative crowd, happy to sit or stand around and watch or compete with the *boules* players in the gritty square opposite. Apart from the show-offs on their souped-up motor bikes, who occasionally roar around the streets, they are well-behaved and not in the least threatening. There is a violent youth problem in some of the more deprived parts of France, but we see little graffiti or gratuitous damage to property in this region, thankfully. You're advised to lock up bikes as they might go 'walkabout' but I feel safe in the streets and in my home. That's more than I can say for London or Guildford.

V7

Limoges powder-bowl

Chapter 16

CULTURE VULTURES

In summer there are countless drama and music festivals in every corner of the Limousin. St Céré hosts a music festival at the end of July and beginning of August. Some performances take place in an old converted factory in town, but the highlights of the season are two operas, staged in the open-air courtyard of the massive fortress of Castelnau-Bretenoux. This triangular red sandstone castle, which dates back to the early 11th century, is visible from miles around and is said to be the second largest fortress in France. The guidebooks don't mention what the largest is!

The barons of Castelnau were the strongest in Quercy and imperiously pronounced themselves the Second Barons of Christendom. In fact they were under the control of the counts of Toulouse who gave away their power over Castlenau to the viscount of Turenne, but the baron refused to be passed on so casually to another feudal lord and declared his allegiance to the King of France, Philip Augustus. Turenne and Castelnau fought bitterly over the situation and it wasn't until the intervention of Philip's successor, Louis VIII, that the dispute was resolved. However, the King declared that instead of the baron of Castelnau being required to provide an army for the service of the viscount of Turenne, as would have been his customary duty, his only fee was to bring him an egg! A freshly-laid egg was duly and ceremoniously delivered to Turenne each year, on a cart pulled by four oxen.

Castelnau-Bretenoux was in a bad way after a fire in 1851 but was rescued and restored by Jean Moulierat, a singer with the Opéra Comique, who bought the castle in 1896. Now in good order, and filled with antiques, including a notable collection of *armoires*, Castelnau has become a magnet for tourists and music lovers. During the festival the small audience is seated on benches, banked up on temporary stands, or on a few rows of hard wooden or plastic chairs at the sides of the simple raised stage. Bringing your own cushion invites envious looks. In the enclosed chateau courtyard the audience is so close to the action that you almost feel part of it. The production in 2001 was a dramatic and moving version of '*Carmen*'. Every smouldering, swaggering look could be minutely observed. It was a strange adaptation: Arab instrumentalists played together with a small group of conventional western musicians. On the whole it worked, conveying the exotic North African influences brought by the Moors to the Andalucian world inhabited by Carmen, her friends and rivals. You were drawn into the mysterious world of the Casbah by clever lighting, with vibrant colours and characters wandering in and out of the shadows. It must have been exhausting to dance flamencos and to sing on such a hot night, in the heavy robes worn by some of the performers. Their flamenco fans were probably wielded in anger that night.

There is an enthusiastic audience for most of the concerts we have attended. The small, cool and simple Romanesque abbey church at Carennac is an excellent venue. Its acoustics are kind to the voice. Whenever I go into an empty church I like to hear whether the acoustics are dry or resonant, and usually try them out with a rendition of the Processional Hodie from Benjamin Britten's Ceremony of Carols. If any one does come into the church I am sure they won't mind, as I am singing a religious piece. Anyway, one evening Pippa, one of her friends and I went to Carennac to hear a German Early Music Consort. We arrived early to reserve good places, and put cushions from Folie on three of the small, hard, rush-seated chairs invariably found in French churches. (Did they design them specially to be uncomfortable so that the congregation would have no chance of going to sleep in the sermon?) Sure of a good position we went to a nearby bar for a drink. On our return we found people sitting on our cushions.

"Excuse me," I said, courteously in French, "Those are our cushions you are sitting on."

"Oh!" said one of the ladies, ingenuously, "We thought that all the seats had cushions and they had been provided for the audience."

A pretty lame excuse, as there were no cushions on any other unoccupied seats; however the ladies were gracious enough to move without further discussion to adjacent chairs. We struck up a pleasant conversation, and settled into our places for an excellent evening of first class music-making. A few days later, we attended another concert in the vast dark nave of the Abbatiale in Beaulieu, this time a performance of folk song and religious works sung by a splendid Russian choir, complete with some fabulous basso-profundo voices. During the interval I spotted the lady from the concert at Carennac. She came over to greet me and with a grin, stated that they had brought their own cushions this time.

I was delighted, on chatting with a Dutch wind band after another summer concert in Carennac, to find that they knew of, and had in fact worked with a harpist who is the daughter of friends from Utrecht. While she was still a student, I adapted an organ piece I had written while still a teenager for her to play, and she liked it well enough to perform it as one of her final examination pieces. I had got to know Ernestine and her family in rather unusual circumstances. As a member of the Bach Choir, in 1971, I was singing in Holland, staying not in hotels but in the homes of musically enthusiastic residents. My hosts, Mr and Mrs Stoop, had a large family of English-speaking musicians. While singing at the Concertgebouwe, I was taken ill and failed to make the second half. As I was pregnant with Pippa, I was most concerned that it was a threatened miscarriage. Very conveniently, Mr Stoop was a doctor, and on examining me said that he thought I might have appendicitis. They organised my return to England, the Bach Choir having moved on and abandoned me! A few days' rest in hospital in England seemed to do the trick and I ended up with both my baby and my appendix. Before leaving Holland, the Stoops insisted I return to stay with them when the baby was born, and the following year Tony and I took Pippa back to see them. Subsequently several of their children came to stay with us to improve their English and to have a holiday. Ernestine went on to have a very successful career as a professional harpist, specialising in contemporary music.

The standard of the musicians at these concerts is generally very high. Many of the performers bring CDs of their recordings for sale. Some local groups, however, don't quite attain this high level, though there are always special moments when the music itself transcends the performers' abilities. Every occasion has its peaks and troughs, and the setting, in fine mediæval or renaissance buildings, usually compensates for any shortcomings. I'm often distracted away from less talented music-making by looking at the weird and wonderful carvings on the capitals, or studying the over-ornate altarpieces. And if those become boring, the audience itself is usually well worth observing. People-watching is one of life's greatest pleasures.

Several important visual artists have lived and worked in

the surrounding towns and villages. Zadkine, a sculptor originally from Russia, settled in Les Arques in the Lot. In his youth
he was influenced by Cubism, but his great variety of styles
showed his constant desire to experiment. Bronzes are sometimes raw and roughcast, whereas others are as smooth and
highly polished. On the walls of a barn, now converted to
house a museum of his work, are drawings, lithographs and
tapestries which show Zadkine's versatility. Most of his forceful and dynamic, semi-abstract carvings represent people,
though some of the sculptures are totally realistic. His later
work is characterised by powerful, thrusting, angular forms,
when his woodcarvings were conceived on a grand scale, more
in the style of the Futurists such as Boccioni and Marinetti,
though he appeared to work quite independently of that
movement. Most sensual of his monumental sculptures is a
very beautiful painted figure of Diana the Huntress, whose
body and hair, the bow, her quiver of arrows and the dog at her
heels all entwine with subtle grace. Each angle from which the
carving can be viewed shows careful planning to give interest
and elegance in every aspect of its form. Within the church
opposite the museum, a painful elongated figure of the cruci-
fied Christ is set high up on the entrance wall. The twisted
body is placed fractionally asymmetrically between the simple
Romanesque windows, while Christ's head is turned to look
up towards heaven, in contrast to most crucifixion figures
whose heads fall forwards. His arms, unsupported by a cross,
appear to stretch up as if to break through the wooden roof
above Him. Les Arques church also contains a very moving
Pietá in the crypt. Like the Diana sculpture, the wood has been
painted in subdued greys and black. Mary is a simple peasant,
her head draped with a shawl. Suffering is all one sees in her
face. She could be mourning the whole world's sorrows as she
cradles the broken figure of her son. Strangely, instead of merely resting on Mary's lap, Jesus' torso is held firm by Mary's left
leg, pinning His body to hers as if she is defending it from further abuse. Jesus' ribs are like an iron cage, one arm lies limply

in Mary's hand, His elbow appears to support his body but His head droops backwards, with open sightless eyes and scarred forehead, the very epitome of death.

The arches inside the church itself are very unusual, as they are horseshoe shaped. Moorish workmen must have penetrated into this part of France from Spain, where their architecture dominates many remarkable cities, and somehow persuaded the designer of Arques church to allow them to create these uncharacteristic arches, more commonly seen in Muslim mosques than in Christian churches. Similar but much smaller Moorish arches are incorporated in the doorway of the church at Collonges la Rouge. Several larger churches, including Beaulieu, Souillac and Perigueux, have domed roofs not unlike those of St Sophia in Istanbul. It is fascinating to consider the great distance travelled by these architectural elements.

The most notable and original tapestry designer to emerge during the 20th century was Jean Lurçat. His workshop having been destroyed by the SS in 1944, he re-established an *atelier* the following year in a house nestling among the 11th century towers of St Laurent which dominate a steep hill above the town of St Ceré in the Lot. This house was a centre for the Resistance during the last year of the war, though Lurçat had been involved with the organisation for longer than that. It is surprising and heartening to read in a biography, found at the back of a lovely illustrated book about his work which I chanced upon in a market, that even during the war years artists were managing to hold exhibitions of their work, not just in their own country but abroad as well. Lurçat shared space with Raoul Dufy at an art gallery in New York in 1942. Now his home has been turned into a museum with some of his finest tapestries. His style does not appeal to everyone, used to the soft gentle colours and flowing curves in the tapestries of earlier centuries. His work is spiky and sharp, and the colours he chose were strong and glowing. Cockerels were a recurrent motif together with all manner of plants. The Coq d'Or Hotel in St Ceré owns several good examples of his work.

There is another museum devoted to his tapestries in Angers, far to the northwest. In Angers castle there is a completely contrasting and immensely long mediæval tapestry devoted to the Apocalyptic Revelations of St John, complete with multiheaded beasts, similar to those carved into the tympanum of the Abbatiale in Beaulieu. This stunning tapestry was found, remarkably undamaged, in a barn not long ago. On one wall of the gallery is a small piece of the tapestry, reversed to show the wrong side where the wool has not been exposed to the light. What it demonstrates is that the colours used hundreds of years ago were originally as bright and vibrant as those we see in Lurçat's work today – not dull and faded at all.

The most celebrated tapestry town is Aubusson, in the Creuse, where wall hangings have been made since the 15th century. At that time the great halls of manor houses were cold and draughty. Little glass was available for general use, and window openings were closed with wooden shutters. Only the few nobs and snobs who could get close to the fire, placed centrally on the hall floor before chimneys were commonplace, were likely to keep warm. Tapestries, covering bare stone walls and hung across doorways, were the only way to keep out the howling winds of winter. No wonder the aristocracy wore furs and velvets, while the poor must have worked hard in their limited spare time weaving rough wool tweed to keep out the cold. Tapestry was still made in Aubusson long after glass was easily obtained and windows could be made much larger than before. Around the turn of the 18th century, designs were frequently copied from the pastoral paintings of Boucher and Watteau, among others. Country scenes, Chinoiserie and flowery patterns were chosen to appeal to a bourgeois society. Rather than the finer silks of the Gobelin factory, wool was used for Aubusson products, including the newly-popular carpets made in the mid 18th century, which were intended for less wealthy clients. Today, however, they fetch vastly inflated prices and, in spite of their modest beginnings, grace many aristocratic houses in England as well as France where they are prized for their decorative value as well as their rarity.

Porcelain and enamelling are the major artistic and commercial products of Limoges. Enamelling on copper using the *cloisonné* technique had its heyday in the 12th century. For this method of enamelling, wires are soldered to the base metal to create small compartments, or *cloisons*, which are then filled with coloured powdered glass, mixed with water, which when fired turns into enamel. The development of this type of decoration dates far back into antiquity. The earliest known examples are some rings, found in a tomb in Cyprus, dating back to the 13th century BC! Considering the complex formula, including silica, potash and various metals needed to produce the colours, let alone the extreme heat required to fuse it onto gold or copper, and the skill to solder the precise designs of the *cloisons*, it is amazing the techniques were ever discovered.

By 1200, Limoges became the centre of the religious reliquary trade, when a new method of production called *champlevé*, had been developed. *Champlevé* was created by cutting away the surface of thick sheets of copper, making deep depressions, sometimes engraved to give added texture, before the enamels were added. Often several layers of enamel were superimposed, giving even greater depth and variety of colour. Large caskets covered in religious scenes in wonderful jewel colours were produced, including a spectacular example made as a shrine for Thomas Becket, now displayed in the Musée de l'Evêché in Limoges. Whether some relic of the Saint was ever contained within it, or indeed is still there, is not mentioned.

The talent for fine detailed painting survived after the decline in the 14th century of the enamelling workshops, to reappear in the porcelain factories. Kaolin, a fine white china clay was discovered locally at Saint-Yrieix, leading to the development from soft to hard porcelain, and the factories of Limoges now account for over 50 per cent of all the porcelain made in France. Delicate scattered flowers and a distinctive subdued gold rim characterises the elegant dishes, dinner services and smaller decorative items made over the last 230 years.

The best quality china is expensive and very beautiful. Along the main roads are drive-in salerooms purporting to sell Limoges china. What are not available in these shops are the pretty feminine pieces usually associated with the name. Mostly the stock in these warehouses is simple plain white tableware of no great merit, or highly decorated small 'collectables', which most people would not be seen dead buying.

Occasionally I have found treasures in the antiques and *brocante* fairs I love to haunt. In the summer, such fairs are held for a day or two in most towns, under the trees in a square or under canvas awnings to protect fine furniture from the scorching sun. Dealers mix with amateurs. Their stalls are not always easy to distinguish. Much of what is on offer is pure junk – cracked plates, stained lace, torn books, wobbly furniture, odd glasses, mousetraps, bits of unidentifiable metal – more like a jumble sale than an antiques fair. I had the good fortune on two occasions to find some lovely Limoges pieces. The first, a flat dish edged with its customary dull gold rim, perfect for serving a large pavlova pudding or hors d'oeuvres, is decorated with scattered flowers, resembling those on a dainty embroidered muslin dress of the early 1800s. It cost about £40 and is now worth a lot more. The other is a flowery powder bowl, influenced by an oriental design which looks like the top of a pagoda. Its eight gently curving sides rise to points, as does the lid, whose curved segments are topped by a golden knob.

Of the more bizarre objects seen at these antiques fairs, a tray of various coloured glass eyes caused a lot of amusement. Lulu and Pippa made us all fall about with laughter as they pretended to be the legendary Cyclops, with one eye in the middle of his forehead. Hats from the 1920s are another source of fun. One looks remarkably old-fashioned in a quaint straw net-draped hat. A dark shawl would easily complete the picture of a lady from the 1920s or '30s. We always hold a competition to find the most grotesque and ghastly object on sale. It often astounds me that someone, somewhere, has actually designed and created these supremely ugly items which triumph in our game. Frequently I see handpainted plates or jugs, and advertising ashtrays similar or identical to those left behind at La Folie Verte by Monsieur Coruble. I have thought about selling some of this stuff but it would not be worth my while to take a stall myself, as the costs are high and although there are many visitors wandering about, few purchases ever seem to be made, especially of the higher priced items. Postcards are popular. Those showing old crafts and people in early 20th century costume fetch the highest prices. £14 for one card is not uncommon. Recently we decided to buy a nicely finished high chair in chestnut wood, which hinges to make a low chair and table, for the princely sum of £20. I have to say that we are not grandparents and bought it purely for decoration, as it is such a nice piece and because it was a bargain. I am always on the lookout for a good bargain, never mind what it is – clothes, furniture, china, jewellery – I hardly buy anything at full price these days.

Linen is probably the best buy. Real linen, embroidered white on white with initials, or trimmed with handmade lace, and striped ticking, fetches less than half the price of such materials at home. However, the sheets are often long and narrower than the usual ones for double beds. Pillowcases are usually square and the linen can be coarse and hard to the touch. Some of it is actually a mixture of cotton and linen. But antique French fabrics are very popular at the moment. You need to be choosy and scrutinise the cloth very critically for repairs and indelible stains. White blouses, lacy or plain, nightwear and petticoats are hung on racks. I love to wear the fine lace-edged and pin-tucked cotton nightdresses. There is nothing more comfortable than sleeping in pure cotton. Often these garments are tight in the armhole, as their previous owners must have been thinner and less muscular than we are today. I am quite used to trying on nighties, to make sure they are big enough, over my tee-shirt in the midst of a market. Nobody gives me a second glance.

Second-hand clothes are bought and sold from mountainous heaps or from garment rails where they are hung up as if they were new. There is a great enthusiasm for 'Retro' clothes and shops selling *braderie* appear in many towns. Most of the clothes are not as good as those given to English jumble sales or charity shops, though a valuable designer outfit can be stumbled upon. At one such stall I bought a good quality leather jacket, only to find the previous owner's Identity Card in an inside pocket. Not something to lose. As my discovery came months after the purchase I have to admit I didn't try to return it.

The stock in antiques shops varies from total junk (*brocante*) to the seriously expensive (*antiquités*), though their names do not always tie up with the prices of the stock. Fortunately, it is often the unwieldy size of a piece of furniture that prevents me from getting carried away in my enthusiasm for a bargain. Smaller objects are less easy to resist. I found 11 matching engraved glasses one day, for a very modest price. After wrapping them the dealer took two pretty unmatching and absolutely filthy wineglasses from the shelf, saying that he would throw them in (well, put them in carefully) for free, as no one else would buy them! Using these, instead of the cheap everyday glasses in the kitchen cupboards at Folie, lends a touch of elegance to even a modest wine. My log bin is a huge copper cauldron, bought from a farmer who deals in a few antiques on the side. Driving anywhere in the countryside may lead to a treasure trove in an old barn or shed. The sign '*Brocante*' will have me diverting suddenly from my intended route up narrow tracks and lanes on the off-chance of a serendipitous purchase. Many towns support a *dépôt de vente*. These are usually run by someone who doubles as a house-clearance and bankrupt stock dealer, who also sells items brought in by the public on a sale or return basis, the shop taking a cut of the profit. Worm-eaten furniture seems to be the predominating feature of these warehouses, though plastic household utensils and hangers are sold cheaply. Occasionally, but not often, a piece of useable furniture can be spotted among the dross.

An alternative to the English system of small charity shops taking over empty premises and selling small-scale goods, is the French network of Emmäus communities. Homeless individuals and families are offered simple accommodation in converted farm buildings in exchange for their services in running large recycling outlets for clothes, books, kitchenwares, electrical goods, bikes and sanitary ware. Furniture is repaired if necessary and sold for sensible prices to support the residents. Assistance is given by charitable professionals, and a new sense of worth engendered in the members. Good use is made of redundant out-of-town properties in this effective self-help scheme. Perhaps we should set up something similar in England. The quality of items for sale is often quite good, and had I room for a fine walnut bedroom suite or chaise longue I could have bought one at a reasonable price many times over.

True antiquities are the heritage of Figeac, at the most southerly range of my territory. The museum there houses relics collected by Champollion, the Egyptologist who deciphered the enigmatic Rosetta Stone, with its inscriptions in Greek, hieroglyphics and a cursive script, which is now in the British Museum. Due to his lengthy and persistent endeavours the enduring riddle of hieroglyphics was solved. His discovery has enabled subsequent Egyptologists to interpret most of the inscriptions known to exist. Champollion returned many times to Egypt to continue his study of the carved texts on tombs and temples before his early death at the age of 42. In the courtyard of Champollion's former home a vast replica of the stone lies on the ground, where it is run and jumped on by countless oblivious children.

A more suitable excursion for children of all ages is to the Museum of Automata at Souillac. There, single figures and groups of musicians take turns in displaying their lifelike actions to music. Some are dancing, playing musical instruments or turning somersaults. Most of the figures are beautifully dressed. A collection of more than 1000 mostly French automata was donated to the museum by the Roullet-Decamps family, one of whom created his first mechanical toy in 1865, a gardener pushing a wheelbarrow. The Bon Marché department store used his skills for an innovative mechanical Christmas window display in 1909. It must have appeared truly magical to both adults and children seeing such amazingly realistic figures moving before their eyes. One of the best exhibits at the museum is the almost full-sized Jazzband of 1920. Its group of black musicians is captivating, if politically incorrect today. A room at the end is devoted to modern mechanical toys and large-scale kinetic constructions. Souillac is perhaps better known culturally for its pineapple-roofed Abbey church, where the old doorway was reversed in the 17th century after it had been mutilated by the Protestants. Its carvings are now visible inside, the most impressive of which is a flowing and sinuous portrayal of the Prophet Isaiah. Considering the interest the French have shown recently in the preservation and restoration of their historical legacy, it is surprising to learn that the rest of the abbey is now a tobacco warehouse.

Fascinating architecture abounds in Quercy, from the grand to the humble. Huge chateaux confront each other across the Dordogne from every vantage point, their dramatic bulk serving as a distant warning to any incautious invaders. Some, however, were built on lower ground and were designed for gracious living rather than defence. Many are open to the curious public, and while many are furnished with fine antiques and tapestries, others are bare and bleak. You are expected to admire the architecture rather than the contents, though more furnished chateaux are now being opened to the public gaze.

There are pretty *pigeonniers* to find and photograph. These buildings are often raised on stilts of brick or stone or the top sections are cantilevered over the pillared base, to deter rats from climbing up. A few of the larger of these structures in romantic locations have been converted to sweet little hideaways. Pippa has always hankered after one. Overlooking the village of Curemonte is a three-storey *pigeonnier*, but I was told that it was unlikely ever to be sold as the young of the village regularly use it for rendezvous, obviously with the connivance of their elders! Many bories, also known as *caselles* or *gariottes*, are found all over the Causses, many near the town of Sarlat. These round stone shelters were perhaps used by farmers to wait until the regular storms that sweep the Corrèze and the Lot had passed over, or maybe they were just for storing tools. No one really knows for sure. The smaller of these bories are about six feet high, their walls gradually curving as the flat overlapping stones form a simple domed roof. Some larger ones have a window and are just about big enough to live in. Similar structures exist in Malta, Turkey and Sardinia, but all of these are thought to be considerably older.

There are numerous fêtes and festivals, when villages celebrate their saints' days with a fair and fireworks. Main streets are closed off with garishly-lit stalls and stands. At Autoire at the beginning of August there is a popular fair, where shooting galleries, 'Catch the Duck', hot dogs and candyfloss, tiny roundabouts and dodgem cars all vie for your attention. A canopied area of the schoolyard is set aside for dancing to an old-fashioned band of local musicians, complete with accordion, who stand at one end on a simple wooden stage. Dancers of all ages take to the floor: grandfathers lead their granddaughters in neat waltzes and quicksteps, girls dance together and shy young men hang around at the edges lecherously eyeing the talent.

One of the more unusual acts I've watched at the fair was a girl whirling a flaming rope over her head, or using it as a skipping rope, flicking it to and fro, making dazzling patterns in the darkness. Her partner conjured with fiery batons. No barriers prevented the audience from standing dangerously close. Safety is not even considered, though the police make their presence felt, as there are likely to be pickpockets among the crowd. Further up the road local *boules* enthusiasts had set up a pitch, but instead of aiming for the jack, one had to throw the balls at three bottles perched on the narrow edge of a plank. I have to say that we English made a better job of knocking them off and breaking them than did some of the French, but maybe they had drunk a few more glasses of beer or wine than we'd had. The cafés all do a lively business on fair days and the alcohol-enhanced atmosphere is noisy, but good-humoured on the whole.

Autoire is set below a remarkable vertiginous inland cliff, left behind by a receding glacier, down which tumbles a 100-foot waterfall. This spectacular cliff and its valley is the setting for one of the most fantastic fireworks shows I have ever seen. At about 11.30pm everyone finds a suitable viewpoint along the road beyond the fair and spends their waiting minutes searching the sky for satellites and shooting stars. Sometimes there is a communal gasp as a particularly dramatic streak pierces the star-sprinkled blackness. The expectant chatter gradually builds until the first enormous 'BOOM' of a firework. Background music suddenly changes to a brilliantly choreographed concert of stirring emotionally-charged music. Caves in the cliffs are lit with coloured fires. Streams of sparks tumble from the rim like waterfalls. Rockets criss-cross and burst, it seems, right above our heads, their twinkling streamers illuminating faces lifted up in wonderment. On one evening balloons wafted away with tiny fireworks suspended beneath. They drifted slowly up the valley, gradually extinguishing as they rose into the night. More rockets, more Roman candles, explosions, fizzing, crackles, bangs, and the last ear-splitting BOOM. The magic has entranced us for a good twenty minutes, and spontaneous applause greets the reluctant end.

I have barely started to explore the almost endless list of fascinating historic towns and villages. In particular, it would be interesting to look closer at the bastide towns, built during the 100 Years War, comparing the English with the French styles, and to research the reasons for their establishment. Some do not appear to be built in good defensive sites at all, so if their purpose was to protect their residents from attack from an enemy, they left themselves rather vulnerable. But if the main purpose was for a knight, of either nationality, to gather more people onto his side and into his army by offering them cheap accommodation in return for their loyalty, you can understand that perhaps the siting of towns as garrisons was less important. Bastides were usually of similar design, whoever built them. A grid pattern of roads, surrounded by strong walls, pierced only by easy-to-defend gateways which led to a central square, usually bordered by arcaded shops. The well-preserved town of Montpazier is an impressive example. The outer walls of Bretenoux lost their defensive value when they were converted into the front walls of houses built right into the earlier fortifications.

Then there are all the fine market squares with their imposing open-sided trading areas to explore. I have yet to visit most of the prehistoric settlements of the Vezère Valley. There are chateaux by the score, which I have not seen. If my French were better I could take advantage of theatrical performances and cinema, though sometimes English language films with French subtitles are shown locally. There is enough of cultural interest in the 50-mile radius around our village to keep all but the most assiduous visitors happy for many years. I have only scratched the surface of what is there to see and could attend a different musical event every evening in the summer, if I so chose. After 14 years I am just a baby vulture, learning to flap her wings.

Chapter 17
THE GOOD LIFE

R esidents of rural France seem to live the good life without really trying. Their needs are few. They work hard when necessary but are content to sit in the sun and take things easy when it's not. If the towns and villages are quiet and restrained, then that is the way people like it. Those young people who want a little excitement can find an out-of-town nightclub. But most appear content to meet friends for a drink, to play *boules* or relax at home. We holiday visitors expect to fill our time rushing around seeing the sights, swimming, canoeing, cycling… busy, busy, busy. But La Folie Verte has a special magic which bewitches all its tenants. It feels quite all right not doing anything much. The daily business of buying groceries and cooking doesn't seem the chore it is at home, and even the men of the family are content to spend most of the morning shopping, particularly if they are allowed to chose some wine or their favourite *pâté* for lunch.

In every direction there are wonderful walks to be enjoyed, around impressive waterfalls or in wooded countryside, with superb views over the river Dordogne, or towards the mountains of the Auvergne. The routes are marked with a system of coloured paint marks on trees, fence posts or telegraph poles, occasionally on the road itself. A straight line means "keep going, you're on the right path". Deviations are indicated with arrows. A cross denotes a road you should not take. Locally available booklets describe many of these walks. Some of the books include hand-drawn plans, often showing the position of places of interest, such as viewpoints, dolmen, interesting geological features or buildings like *pigeonniers* and watermills. However, we always take a detailed local map as well, as occasionally the descriptions are wrong and sometimes the paint marks are nowhere to be seen, the posts having fallen over or the ivy grown so thick they've been obscured. I suppose we should really carry a compass, but as most of the paths twist and turn around the hills it might be more confusing than helpful. Fortunately the mistakes we make generally seem to shorten our journey rather than lengthen it. A good 'nose' for the right general direction is an advantage.

An even simpler pleasure is just to sit and stare 'people-watching' from a bench or a café. People are always fascinating to observe. We love to fantasise about their lives and make up little stories about what they do and how they live.

In France one is never hurried away from a table outside a bar. You can sit with one drink just as long as you want. Your presence makes the café look busy and brings in more customers. It is noticeable that many coffee bars have opened in England in the last few years, some of them comfortably furnished with sofas and armchairs to encourage the customers to stay longer, and there are increasingly more cafés with tables outside. In England you probably still buy a second cup of coffee as you feel a bit guilty occupying a seat for a long time, if

In France one is never hurried away from a table outside a bar

you've only come in to meet friends and have a chat. This sense of guilt doesn't seem to occur to the French café table occupier.

Corrèze is one of the most backward areas of France, particularly the isolated and under-populated area called Xaintrie, off the tourist itinerary. This insular plateau, lost between the rivers Dordogne and Cère, with its ancient, scattered communities among high farmland and forests, has some amusingly named villages. They seem particularly funny to us if they are pronounced in a very English accent. How about Sexcles (Anne's family calls it sexicals, which they think sounds like something rude that has to be strapped on!). Then there are Goulles and St Privat.

Xaintrie also has a high concentration of inbred inhabitants, so sadly there are a number of people whom we would formerly have described as 'simple'. They are an accepted and visible part of most communities and their presence, as they stand for hours on a street corner or shamble along, muttering quietly and incomprehensibly under their breath, excites no interest or obvious concern. Instead of being shuffled off into a home, they are, like the old folk, just another part of the daily scene.

I met one old lady in our village, who'd crossed the road from her house to see what I was painting. She lived in a tiny two or three-roomed house opposite the church. After a few minutes of sociable conversation she tottered back to her cottage, returning with a photo of a wonderful old house, very large, standing in its own grounds high on a hill some miles away, which she said was her home. She had moved to this tiny house in the village to be near her friends, the *boulangerie*, and the little square where the grocery van stopped twice a week, so she could continue to be independent of her family. I think she must then have been well over eighty, fiercely determined not to be a burden on her relations, and she was managing perfectly well under the watchful eye of her kindly neighbours. In England she would have been shunted into an old people's home and forgotten.

The extended family still has its place in these close-knit rural communities. Although the village school which used to occupy part of the Mairie has closed, there are still children who take a school bus to Beaulieu and who live in close proximity to their grandparents. Teenagers drive mopeds and, as soon as they can afford it, cars, to college or work, often having to go the twenty miles to Brive to find a job. But most still live at home until they marry.

For me, one of life's pleasures is painting and drawing. I don't need much equipment for watercolour painting, though I usually have a lightweight stool in the car in case there isn't a handy doorstep or wall to sit on.

Everywhere in Folie's environs there are picturesque subjects. I prefer not to be overlooked or have people talking to me while I work; though if I choose a popular village to paint in I have to put up with observers. It is often said, by those who do not paint, that it must be a wonderfully relaxing hobby. If you live a hectic life, commuting and running a business, then painting is certainly a way to switch off, but it's hardly relaxing. It requires a great deal of concentration to draw perspective accurately, and to mix the right colours.

When I was teaching Art, I would tell my mature students that painting was 80 per cent looking and 20 per cent doing – you look at the subject, draw a line, look again to see if it was right, then look again before making the next mark.

Working in colour is even more time-consuming, as you look, mix a colour, look again to see if the colour is right, paint the little patch of colour on the paper and look again at the subject to see if it is OK, and if not, start again and mix another colour, for another layer. If you want a bit of peace and quiet, with the possibility of producing something pleasing to look at and having done so, can feel the glow of achievement, then painting in a secluded corner is the thing, even if it is not 100 per cent relaxing.

So what is the great appeal of a holiday house in France? Creating somewhere attractive and comfortable on a budget?

Eating well and drinking even better? Getting away from the eternal telephone and compulsive television? Enjoying a less pressured way of life? Touring on uncluttered roads? Or just relaxing in the sun? All of these! So go there, buy your own house and you will find your own reasons.

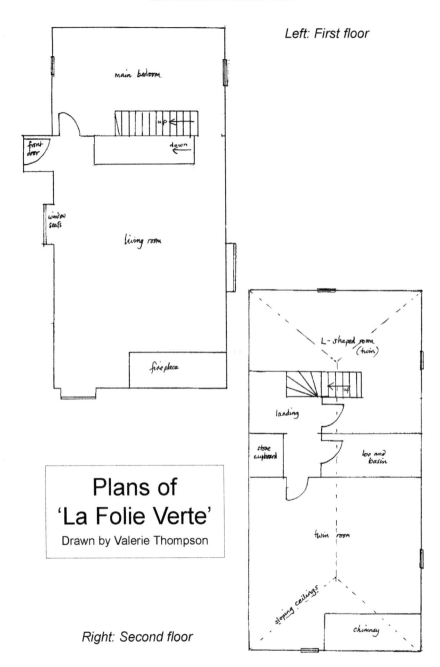

Left: First floor

Plans of
'La Folie Verte'
Drawn by Valerie Thompson

Right: Second floor

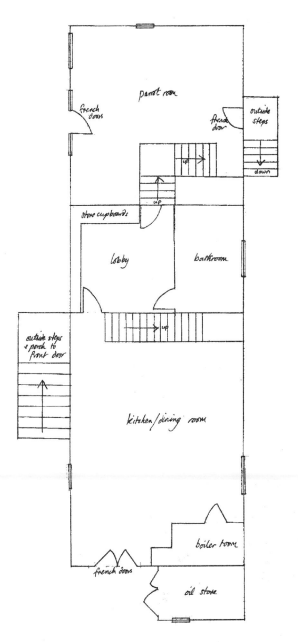

Above: Ground floor

Some of the French-based books
published by the Léonie Press:

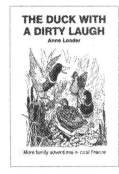

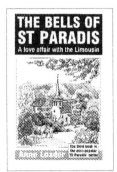

A BULL BY THE BACK
DOOR
by ANNE LOADER

THE DUCK WITH A DIRTY
LAUGH by ANNE LOADER
ISBN 1 901253 0 90 £8.99

THE BELLS OF ST PARADIS
by ANNE LOADER
ISBN 1 901253 26 0 £9.99

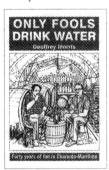

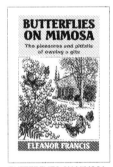

ONLY FOOLS DRINK WATER
by GEOFFREY MORRIS
ISBN 1 901253 10 4 £8.99

OU EST LE 'PING'?
by GRACE McKEE
ISBN 1 901253 11 2 £7.99

BUTTERFLIES ON MIMOSA
by ELEANOR FRANCIS
ISBN 1 901253 23 6 £8.99

LILAC AND ROSES
by PEGGY ANDERSON
ISBN 1 901253 22 8 £8.99

BANANAS IN BORDEAUX
LOUISE FRANKLIN CASTANET
ISBN 1 901253 29 5 £10.99

POLLY TAKES THE SCENIC
ROUTE by GAY PYPER
ISBN 1 901253 33 3 £8.99